Richard Wigginton Thompson

Recollections of Sixteen Presidents from Washington to Lincoln

Richard Wigginton Thompson

Recollections of Sixteen Presidents from Washington to Lincoln

ISBN/EAN: 9783744720861

Printed in Europe, USA, Canada, Australia, Japan

Cover: Foto ©Suzi / pixelio.de

More available books at **www.hansebooks.com**

RECOLLECTIONS

OF

SIXTEEN PRESIDENTS

FROM

WASHINGTON TO LINCOLN

BY

RICHARD W. THOMPSON

"Let us forget party and think of our country. That country embraces both parties. We must endeavor, therefore, to serve and benefit both. This can not be effected while political delusions array good men against each other."—GOUVERNEUR MORRIS.

" Three-score and ten I can remember well;
Within the volume of which time I have seen
——————————things strange."
—SHAKESPEARE.

VOLUME II

INDIANAPOLIS

THE BOWEN-MERRILL COMPANY

1894

CHAPTER XI

JAMES K. POLK

DURING Polk's administration the public patience was severely tried. All protestations against the violation of the Constitution were answered by the roar of cannon and the deafening shouts of maddened partisans, who seemed to suppose that patriotism consisted only in a clamorous demand for enlarging the borders of the nation, no matter whether the means employed were right or wrong. The history of that period, therefore, should be well and carefully studied, in order to understand by what strange combinations a man of mere mediocre ability and without national reputation for statesmanship became enabled to defeat Van Buren—the acknowledged choice of Jackson —and reached the Presidential office. I do not contest, in the least degree, the claim he had upon his friends for such respectful consideration as should never be withheld from a well-spent private life, but can not refrain from asserting that, in my opinion, his intellectual qualifications never exceeded the average among public men. One of his confidential friends, from his own State, whose good and generous qualities won my personal esteem, wrote a history of his administration, in which he referred to his election as "indeed remarkable." This expressed the general sentiment. That he discharged his official duties

16 (241)

industriously, was well attested, but that he possessed the qualities which entitled him to be classed among American statesmen of commanding ability, was not claimed for him even by his most zealous defenders. The highest round he reached in the ladder of fame was that of respectability—nothing more. His nomination for the Presidency took the whole country by surprise, and by none of the people more than those of Tennessee, among whom he had lived nearly all his life. The Legislature of that State had, without any indication of enthusiasm, nominated him for the Vice-Presidency, but this met no response from any other part of the country, and was considered as merely complimentary. There was no popular demonstration in his favor even for this office. In view, therefore, of all the attending circumstances, his nomination for the Presidency can be viewed in no other light than as the result of political maneuvering upon the part of those who had some secret object to accomplish, and who, in order to assure success, were indifferent regarding the means they employed.

No sooner had Tyler indicated the purpose to bring about the annexation of Texas, in order to recover somewhat the popularity his administration had lost, than a class of politicians, both in the North and the South, conceived the idea of circumventing him by strategy, so as to take the matter out of his hands and transfer it to their own—that is, in common phrase, to steal his thunder. This purpose was soon manifested by their opposition to his annexation treaty, but afterwards became more palpable when they endeavored to denationalize the question by narrowing it to a controversy between the sections for political supremacy. In order to accomplish this their first and chief contrivance was so to present the question as to make the approaching Presidential nominations dependent upon it—that is, to give it such prominence as to dwarf all other political questions. Hence the opinions of the Presidential aspirants were sought after. There were but two of these—Van Buren and Clay—each of whom was recognized as the representative of his party. The former had the indorsement of Jackson, whose fidelity to the Union was vouched for by the policy of his own administration, and the latter had multitudes of friends who were tied to him by a chord of sympathy which passed from him to them like an electric current. The two represented all the varieties of political sentiment then supposed to be involved in a Presidential contest, even the most minute differences of opinion. To repeat, each was the acknowledged representative of his party and would have remained so had it not been for the method these scheming politicians adopted to multiply the sources of disaffection between the sections in order to assure the increase of the slave power and keep the government under their control. In answer to the interrogatories put to them they agreed in opposing the *immediate* annexation of Texas, but for different reasons, which are of no present consequence. Each expressed his opinion unequivocally. Van Buren's letter was dated April 20, 1844, a little over a month before the meeting of the nominating convention held by those with whom he had been accustomed to act. This gave time enough to formulate a plan of opposition to him so as to secure his defeat, although up to that time his nomination had been generally conceded, more especially because it was understood that Jackson desired it. This plan was secretly and cautiously contrived by those well skilled in that particular method of procedure —adepts in the art—but it was not developed until the nominating convention met, May 27, 1844, and then only by the false pretense of fairness, set up and persisted in on purpose to gain an undue advantage. As it was the first time in our history when the minority openly obtained the mastery over the majority, and the authority it then acquired has been perpetuated until the present time, it is still necessary that the precise method of proceeding shall be thoroughly exposed. Wrongs do not right themselves, and unless brought to light are apt to perpetuate their bad influences for an indefinite period.

The projectors of this scheme, to take the choice of a Presidential candidate out of the hands of the majority, where it had been popularly lodged as a safeguard against imposture, were successful in their first effort—which was to require two-thirds, instead of a majority, of the votes of the convention to make a nomination. Of course such a proposition was at first objected to, for reasons which will readily occur to all intelligent minds, but the expediency of winning success was more potent than the obligation to preserve a fundamental principle, hitherto considered inviolate. Notwithstanding it was entirely new in American politics, the convention, after an animated and somewhat violent struggle, was persuaded to accept it, possibly without the suspicion upon the part of the majority of the result designed to be accomplished by it. However this may have been, it put winning cards in the hands of the *immediate* annexationists, who were too sagacious and too well trained not to know that, with a consolidated South upon their side, they could con-trol the nomination, because, although a majority could, the necessary two-thirds could not, be acquired in the di-vided North. And they calculated rightly—understand-ing perfectly well that the desire for success was to such a degree the controlling impulse of the convention that but little regard was paid to the means of obtaining it. The convention remained in session three days, all of which were days of excitement. There were plottings and counter-plottings, and it required nine ballots to produce a nomination, notwithstanding Van Buren had no avowed competitor, and was, besides, the favorite of Jackson, who, although in retirement at the Hermitage, was so influential that the conspiring malcontents were afraid of open opposition to the candidate of his choice, and insidiously carried on the plan of opposition to him by the invention of the two-thirds rule. Upon the first three ballots Van Buren received, respectively, 146, 127 and 121 votes, while the remaining votes were scattered among five others, none of whom had been put in nom-ination, and who, consequently, were not candidates. Upon either of these three ballots Van Buren, having re-ceived a majority of the votes, would have been nom-inated but for the two-thirds rule, which was in direct conflict with the universal American custom and the spirit of our popular institutions. It was not intended, how-ever, that he should be nominated, or any other man who refused to put himself under the complete dominion of the faction who were plotting against the majority,

and, therefore, against the fundamental principles upon
which popular government rests.   Everything that occurred proves this.   Van Buren began to fall off after the
first ballot, and Cass, who had not been known as a candidate, ran ahead of him upon the fifth, sixth, seventh
and eighth ballots—having also received a majority of the
votes, that is, 123, on the seventh ballot.   But the minority were no better satisfied with Cass than with Van
Buren, because he was not committed to *immediate* annexation, and steadfastly adhering to their resolution not
to permit a nomination until they could procure a candidate obedient to themselves, despite the majority, they
continued to scatter their votes among those who were
not candidates.   At this stage of the proceedings, and
upon the eighth ballot, Polk was brought forward for the
first time by those who had previously rallied under the
flag of "Texas or disunion."   His opinion had not been
sought by letter, as that of Van Buren had, but they
knew him well enough to know they could trust him,
more especially as they had the power to demonstrate by
another ballot that he would be nominated, if at all,
from a slave State, while Van Buren and Cass were defeated after each had received a majority, because they
were both from free States.   Accordingly, upon the eighth
ballot, Van Buren received 104 votes, Cass 114, Buchanan 2, Calhoun 2 and Polk 44.   The effect of this was
exactly what was designed, that the New York friends
of Van Buren became indignant at the discovery of the
trick played upon them by the two-thirds rule, and
withdrew his name, declining to have him sacrificed at
the behest of a factional and sectional minority.   Then

the question became one of the utmost magnitude—
whether to permit this minority to dictate the selection of
Polk, or dissolve the convention without making a nomination. After much wrangling and tribulation, the majority yielded to the minority—preferring that to dissolution—and Polk was nominated on the next, or ninth, ballot, not unanimously, but by a vote of 233, with 31 cast
against him. At no nomination ever made for the Presidency was there so much general surprise.

To call a result thus produced a compromise, is to deal
with it much too mildly. It was nothing less than compulsion, in the extremest sense. And when those who
had ruled the convention by means of the two-thirds rule
discovered that it was likely to be so regarded by
thoughtful and considerate people—some of whom were
in the convention and courageous enough to express
their disapprobation—they endeavored to appease the
rising wrath of the friends of Van Buren and Cass, by
nominating Silas Wright, one of the most distinguished
and confidential friends of the former, for Vice-President.
In addition to this motive, which was too palpable to be
disguised, it was understood that the nomination of
Wright, he being from New York, was an effort to con-
ciliate those of the North who supposed the Union to
have been formed for other objects than merely to
strengthen the slave power. But the scheme failed at
this point to bear the fruits expected from it, for Wright
promptly and peremptorily refused to become a party to
it by declining the nomination. It was understood that
he considered it as insidiously aimed at his friend Van
Buren and as likely to be fraught with mischief to the

country; and in order to give more significance to the course he felt constrained to pursue, he voted in the Senate, less than two weeks after, against the treaty for annexing Texas. After he declined to play the part assigned to him, George M. Dallas was nominated for Vice-President, and the convention adjourned, greatly to the discomfiture of Van Buren and his friends, but to the undisguised joy of those who were devoting their energies to strengthening the slave power by the *immediate* annexation of Texas. In the whole movement this was the primary and governing incentive, while the interest of Texas was entirely secondary and incidental.

By the platform of this convention "the *re*-occupation of Oregon, and the *re*-annexation of Texas at the earliest practicable period," were insisted upon in the most emphatic terms, as if, in point of fact, we had been wrongfully deprived of the former by Great Britain, and of the latter by Mexico. These two propositions thus became actual and affirmative issues, while the remainder of the platform was a repetition of the negations which had tied the hands of Van Buren and caused his defeat four years before. Upon these latter, however, great stress was laid by the State-rights and strict-construction party of the South, because, by their theory of government, the States would be increased in power to whatever extent that of the nation was weakened; and by this means these factional leaders of the South would, it was hoped, be able to regain what they had lost in their controversy with Jackson,—that is, the right to nullify all such laws of the United States as they might, regardless of national affairs, consider in conflict with their own local and sectional interests. If they could succeed in increasing the slave power by the *immediate* annexation of Texas—the capital prize in the political lottery upon which their hopes were centered—they were willing to remain in quietude for the time being; and in order to assure themselves of this, they contrived the two-thirds rule, in order to prevent a nomination by the convention until they became masters of the situation. Consequently, when they obtained the nomination of Polk, they dictated the negative platform of 1844, with the special design—if Texas were annexed and the slave power strengthened—of so resisting the National Government that its enactments should be "the supreme law of the land" only when it pleased the slave States to recognize them as such. To carry out this purpose effectually they declared that the Constitution should be "strictly construed"—meaning thereby that nothing should be inferred in behalf of the nation, but that everything deemed necessary by the States should be inferred in their behalf; in other and apter words, that the nation should be reduced to a mere confederation and so shorn of its powers as to be made dependent, even for its existence, upon the consent of rival States rather than upon that of the aggregated millions whose "general welfare" it was intended to protect and advance.

Accordingly, they denied the power of Congress to make appropriations for internal improvements, manifestly hoping to keep the treasury in such a condition of repletion as to furnish the means to extend the slave power by procuring Texas. They denied its power to pay the debts of the States, although no such proposition existed except in their own imagination, which denial would undoubtedly have been excluded if they had foreseen the complications which made them powerless to resist the demand of Texas for the payment of her debt. They denied the power to foster one branch of industry at the expense of another, an illusion which originated with those who imagined their own prosperity would be promoted by making up the difference between the value of free and slave labor by reducing the former to a common level with the latter. They denied the power to charter a national bank with as much apparent complacency as if Washington and Madison and the Supreme Court of the United States and numerous Congresses and the people had not repeatedly affirmed the existence of that power and the necessity for its exercise when demanded for the development of our domestic and foreign commerce. They denied the power to interfere with the domestic institutions of the States, meaning slavery, well knowing that even the abolitionists did not claim the existence of any such power, and that if one who did could be found here and there in the North he was frowned upon by the multitude and stood a fairer chance to be struck by lightning than he did to obtain a political office. Summing up these allegations it is easy now to see, when the passions of that period have been buried in the graves of the chief disturbers of the public peace, that they were designed to reduce the National Government into absolute inferiority to the States, and to confer authority upon the latter to terminate the existence of the former whenever it denied the right of a factious and sectional minority to subordinate the "general welfare" to their own. Seeming, however, to realize that a national government of exclusively negative authority would be powerless in the presence of the other nations or for self-preservation, they conceded to it only the powers to practice economy, as if this were not the subject especially selected by demagogues for the exhibition of their highest powers of oratory; to maintain the principles of the Declaration of Independence—as if anybody, man, woman or child, desired to set it aside; and to defend and preserve the President's *veto* power—as if that kingly prerogative were absolutely necessary to enable one man to defeat the will of the people and protect them against themselves. Hence, it requires nothing more than average intelligence to see that instead of there having been enumerated in this platform upon which Polk was required to stand, such affirmative powers as the government had been accustomed to exercise since the administration of Washington, and which had assured the growth, prosperity and development of the country, it expressly denied the most important of those powers, leaving them to exist in the State governments or not at all. The platform was, consequently, entirely negative, except in so far as it affirmed the power to *re*-occupy Oregon and *re*-annex Texas—in other words, the acquisition of foreign territory. And thus are plainly and palpably shown the objects intended to be accomplished by Polk's nomination, objects which can be better comprehended when the methods adopted to secure his election are understood, so that a rule may be supplied for interpreting the most prominent measures of his administration.

It was but four years before the time of Polk's candidacy when the abolitionists—or liberty party, as they called themselves—began to assume consequence enough to exercise active influence in a contest for the Presidency. They nominated James G. Birney for President in 1840, and he failed to receive a single electoral vote. Out of 2,413,848 popular votes but 7,059 were cast for him,—so small a portion as to prove to all dispassionate people that no actual danger to the institution of slavery in any single State was threatened. In the North this movement was considered so visionary that it did not create the least agitation of political affairs. But in the South it was strangely magnified into such undue importance that it gave "aid and comfort" to sectional agitators, who defiantly arraigned the whole North for sympathy with it, and allowed their misguided zeal to outstrip their discretion in inflammatory appeals to sectional passion. They stamped their feet with mock indignation upon the most irrefragible proofs that slavery was not in danger, because if the sectional discord they purposely stirred up had died out their occupation, like Othello's, would have been gone. The election of Polk, as the forerunner of the immediate annexation of Texas, was the stake they played for; and for this they labored to solidify the South both by fear and hope;—fear of Northern aggression, and the hope of acquiring slave territory enough to add four or five new slave States to the Union. This acted reciprocally upon the abolitionists, who, realizing that foreign territory could only be acquired by following precedents which violated the Constitution, re-nominated Birney upon a platform consisting of a long string of impracticable platitudes. And thus these rival factions—for sectionalism is necessarily factional—forced upon the conservative masses of both sections an issue calculated and designed to inflame the passions and put an end to calm discussion. Each fought with weapons forged in the red-hot furnace of sectional animosity.

Another convention nominated Tyler as his own successor. This had no other visible effect than to excite the apprehension that it would likely weaken Polk in several States to such an extent as to promise his defeat. Tyler was fully aware of this advantage and did not hesitate to avow his resolution to maintain his position, at least until he became assured of his ability to dictate such terms of surrender as were satisfactory to himself and not injurious to those he designated as his friends. Polk himself soon became aware of the actual condition of affairs, and personally engaged in an effort to get Tyler out of the way, as the latter could not take a single vote from Clay—the only competitor he dreaded—but might take enough from him to insure his defeat. And here we reach a point in American politics wholly without parallel, in so far as it involves the direct individual and personal agency of a Presidential candidate. The details would now be rejected as incredible, if they were not attested by the highest and best authority—that is, by Thomas H. Benton, in his "Thirty Years in the United States Senate," where all the facts are given with particularity of detail.

The *Globe* newspaper, published by Blair and Rives in Washington City, was the "organ" of Jackson's and of Van Buren's administrations. Blair, the editor, was not only a man of irrepressible energy but a writer of great power. He was perfectly familiar with political history and fearless in his method of discussing public questions. During Jackson's controversy with the nullifiers of South Carolina he had denounced them with his accustomed severity, and had become especially odious to Calhoun in consequence of his fierce attacks upon him as their great leader and patron. The *Globe* had been continued under Tyler's administration, but Tyler had an organ of his own, called the *Madisonian*, which shone with an exceedingly dim light by the side of it. As Blair—who was devoted to Jackson and zealous in his defense—refused to become reconciled to nullification any more under Tyler than he had been under Jackson, the nullifying friends of Calhoun considered it important that he should be got rid of in some way. To accomplish this, says Benton, "it was in the month of August, 1844, that a leading citizen of South Carolina, and a close friend of Mr. Calhoun,—one who had been at the Baltimore Presidential convention, but not in it—arrived at *Mr. Polk's residence in Tennessee*, had interviews with him, and made known the condition on which the vote of South Carolina for him might be dependent." In order that this proposition shall be understood it should not be forgotten that the electoral vote of South Carolina was cast by the Legislature and not by the people, so that it could be easily sold and delivered to whomsoever contributed efficient support to the cause of nullification, and to no other. Consequently, the proposition made directly and personally to Polk by this friend of Calhoun simply pointed out to him the condition upon which he could obtain the support of the nullifiers of South Carolina and the electoral vote of that State. The condition was this, that Polk, if elected, should "discontinue Mr. Blair as the organ of the administration,"—should discard the old and true friend of Jackson, who hated nullification as intensely as Jackson did, and put in his place one who better understood how to gloss over with smoother words the crime of rebellion. Benton continues: "Mr. Polk was certain of the vote of the State if he agreed to the required condition; AND HE DID SO." The transaction was simple—wholly free from complications—and all its details were easily understood. It was nothing more nor less than an offer to sell the electoral vote of a State, and the acceptance of the offer by the chief beneficiary—himself a Presidential candidate! True, this acceptance involved a political alliance with the most vindictive and violent enemies Jackson ever had, at the time when they were accustomed to round off some of their most eloquent and impassioned periods in defaming him. How well it verifies the old adage—"politics makes strange bedfellows!" All the parties would have made apt disciples of the great Talleyrand, the political magician of France; or, it may be, he could have learned from them some instructive lessons in dissimulation.

Tyler was hostile to Blair because the *Globe* had attacked him and his administration; and Calhoun, his Secretary of State, reciprocated this feeling, because the same paper, in its defense of Jackson, had characterized nullification as treason. The contrivers of this conspiracy knew all these things, as they also knew that Tyler's passions

could be played upon to their profit, if he could be approached properly by one who, like Polk, might have it in
his power to benefit either him or his friends. Tyler had
himself tried to induce the *Globe* to change its course toward his administration by '' a printing job of $20,000,''
but Blair was inexorable and could not be purchased.
'' It now became,'' says Benton, '' the interest of Mr.
Polk to assist Mr. Tyler in punishing, or silencing that
paper; AND IT WAS DONE.'' The first necessary step was
''to get Mr. Tyler out of the way of Mr. Polk,'' by getting
''Mr. Blair out of the way of Mr. Tyler.'' What a field
for the display of strategic genius, upon the part of
two American politicians, one of whom actually filled the
Presidential office, and the other was plotting to obtain
it! Polk, from the beginning, was anxious, of course,
to get Tyler out of his way, and became equally anxious
to get Blair out of the way also, after the visit of Calhoun's South Carolina friend, because nine electoral
votes were dependent upon it—a most important factor
in a Presidential election he then considered by no means
certain. As matters progressed, the two objects—getting rid of both Tyler and Blair—grew in importance
and seemed more united together; for we learn from
Benton that one '' who afterwards became a member of
his [Polk's] cabinet, wrote to him in July, that the main
obstacle to Mr. Tyler's withdrawal was the course of the
Globe towards him and his friends;'' and another friend
urged him by all means ''to devise some mode of in-
ducing Mr. Tyler to withdraw.'' Everything was conducted in the utmost secrecy and was strictly confidential,
as it was absolutely necessary to conceal it from the sin-

cere friends of Jackson,—for if the "old hero" had discovered that Polk was scheming to be made President by a combination with the nullifiers, and with Calhoun at their head, no power upon earth would have been sufficient to prevent him from denouncing them before the nation;—in which event Polk would have stood about an equal chance of being chosen Sultan of Turkey as he would to have been elected President.

It was easier to plan than to execute the scheme to get rid of Blair or silence the *Globe*. There was no direct method of accomplishing either, for neither Blair nor Rives could be intimidated. Therefore, another project was concocted, which was to purchase the *Globe* and convert it into a paper that should defend Tyler's administration specially including the Department of State under the management of Calhoun, and to advocate Polk's election! To execute this purpose was no easy matter, for the *Globe* establishment was of great value—either more than the "allied powers" could raise, or, if they could, than they were disposed to risk upon an adventure so hazardous. Being so desperately bent, however, upon accomplishing their object, and having learned how effectively "the ropes" which led into and out of the national treasury could be handled by dexterous fingers, they prevailed upon the Secretary of the Treasury to cause $50,000 of the public money to be transferred to an obscure bank in Pennsylvania, at a point where no public money was disbursed, so that it could be made available for the purchase of the *Globe*. Steps were then taken by those who controlled this obscure bank to notify "a gentleman in Tennessee," who was Andrew Jackson Donelson, that

17

this $50,000 could be made available for "establishing a new government organ in Washington City," of which he could be made the editor, and requesting him "to come on to Washington for the purpose." Donelson was offended by this proposition and indignantly made the transaction known to Jackson, whose private secretary he had been. Benton says: "His (Jackson's) generous and high blood boiled with indignation at what seemed to be a sacrifice of Mr. Blair for some political consideration, for the letters were so written as to imply a *recognition on the part of Mr. Polk* and of two persons who were to be members of his cabinet," which latter fact shows how well and sagaciously the plan must have been laid, when the services of prominent public men were secured in aid of such an undertaking by the promise beforehand that they should become cabinet officers in the event of success! If Jackson had been informed of the combination with the nullifiers personally made by Polk in order to secure the electoral vote of South Carolina his wrath would have been far greater and more violent than it was. But as this had not been communicated to Donelson, nor by him to Jackson, the latter had knowledge only of the efforts in progress to obtain the *Globe* and get Blair out of the way. He accordingly wrote immediately to Blair and informed him of what was going on, telling him also that the original plan was, in the event that Donelson should decline the editorship of the new organ, that Ritchie, of the *Richmond Enquirer*, in Virginia, should be selected for that purpose. Jackson also informed Polk what he had learned from Donelson and expressed plainly to him his disapproval of the demoralizing scheme. What afterwards occurred beyond this between the parties immediately engaged, with reference to further preliminaries, has not been exposed, and, of course, never will be. The following facts, however, have become historical:—that, notwithstanding Jackson's protest, the conspirators consummated ˉtheir purposes in spite of him; the $50,000 of public deposits were used to purchase the *Globe*; Blair having been induced to sell, laid down his editorial pen and was silenced. The *Union* newspaper was established in place of the *Globe* as the organ of the combination and advocate of Polk's election. Ritchie became its editor; Tyler withdrew as a candidate for President in favor of Polk, the conditions of the alliance between Polk and the nullifiers agreed upon at the beginning of the canvass with the "leading citizen" of South Carolina were fulfilled, and the nine electoral votes of that State were cast for him, and Polk and Dallas were elected over Clay and Frelinghuysen. And now, after the lapse of nearly half a century, when the chief actors are insensible alike to praise or censure, these startling facts are revived for the purpose only of stimulating the popular vigilance and suggesting that, in its absence, our institutions are in perpetual danger of being placed in serious peril by the machinations of those who suffer their ambitious longings after power to become their controlling impulse. Among the lessons of universal history there is not one more impressively taught than this—that the walls of the strongest fortress may be undermined when the watchmen are asleep.

The election by which Polk acquired the Presidency in 1844 shows, in a striking degree, the working of our elective system.   The whole popular vote cast was 2,698,-611.   Of this Polk received 1,337,243; Clay, 1,299,-068, and Birney, 62,300.   As the total vote cast for Clay and Birney was 1,361,368, it will thus be seen that Polk was 12,062 votes short of a majority, and, consequently, in so far as the votes of the people were concerned, be-came the President of the minority, and not of the ma-jority.   A like result followed the election in the State of New York.   There 485,881 votes were cast, of which Polk received 237,588; Clay, 232,481, and Birney, 15,-812.   Hence, he had but a plurality of only 5,352 over Clay, while he fell 10,705 short of the majority.   Yet the thirty-six electoral votes of that State were cast for him because of this small plurality, whereas, if it had been withheld in obedience to a decision of the majority, the election of President would have devolved upon the Con-gressional House of Representatives.   Although, there-fore, he legally became President, notwithstanding a majority of the votes were cast against him, neither he nor his friends were justified in inferring, as they did, that his election was an approval of the *immediate* annex-ation of Texas, because, as Clay and Birney were both opposed to that policy, and their joint vote exceeded his by 12,062, it was condemned by that majority—not very large, it is true, but, nevertheless, an actual majority. The responsibility for the violation of the popular will, by the defeat of Clay, rests upon the friends of Birney—for if the latter had not been a candidate Clay would un-doubtedly have been elected, and many of the disastrous consequences which have since ensued—injurious alike to all sections of the country—would have been escaped.   If

there had then been given to the popular verdict the influence to which it is entitled under our institutions, the *immediate* annexation of Texas would have been defeated,
and that territory might have been annexed long ago by
peaceful and quiet methods—the war with Mexico would
not have occurred—and it is reasonably certain that our
devastating civil war would have been avoided. Instead,
however, of obeying the popular will, the parties to the
alliance between Tyler and Polk, which had elected the
latter, plunged heedlessly into a series of measures which,
in the end, and through terrible sufferings and travail,
produced the very result they sought to prevent—breaking the bonds of every slave in the land. How well they
verified the truth of the old adage, ''Whom the gods
seek to destroy they first make mad.''

The joint resolution for annexing Texas did not pass
the Senate until March 1, 1845, but Tyler approved it
the same day. It provided that *the government* should
settle the boundary between Texas and Mexico,—re-
served to Texas her immense body of ''vacant and un-
appropriated lands,'' for the specified purpose of en-
abling her to pay her ''debts and liabilities,'' and with
the right after that was done to dispose of the remainder
as she pleased,—and with the ultimate object of creating four other States out of her territory, to be free or
slave as the people thereof should decide, below 36° 30'
of north latitude, and to be free above that line. This
latter provision, however, was inserted for mere form's
sake, and had the effect only of committing all the supporters of annexation to the principle afterwards embodied in what was known as the '' Wilmot Proviso,'' by

which the constitutional power to prevent the introduction of slavery into the Territories of the United States was expressly asserted. After Polk became President other steps were taken in Texas, such as the formation and adoption of a constitution, and the State was not regularly admitted into the Union until December 27, 1845. It is proper, however, to remark in this connection, that the debt of Texas was indicated by her bonds, called "Texas Scrip." But it did not take her long to discover that she was unable to pay them, notwithstanding her immense body of vacant lands; and the consequence was that this scrip, thrown upon the market, became almost valueless and was bought up by speculators at a merely nominal price. These speculators had no difficulty in causing Texas to represent to Congress her inability to pay her debt, and to solicit the United States to do so. It required some time and skillful management to accomplish this, but it was done at last by an act of Congress, approved August 2, 1850, whereby it was provided that the United States should pay to Texas $10,000,000 in bonds, payable in 1864, and drawing five per cent. interest. By this operation immense fortunes were made by the holders of the Texas bonds, and Texas was permitted to retain the ownership of all her lands, except what was supposed to be about 100,000 square miles surrendered to New Mexico, and which was pretended to be the consideration for the principal and interest of these government bonds, which, when paid, amounted to the aggregate sum of $17,000,-000. The greater part of the territory thus surrendered was, and still is, barren and arid, and, if ever sold, will not produce money enough to pay the expenses of the surveys and sales. This left Texas with about 270,000 square miles, or 172,800,000 acres, of territory—whereas the States of Ohio, Indiana, Illinois and Iowa, united, contain but little more than this, and have always been required to pay their own debts. And, besides, the friends of annexation, in order to produce that result, nominated Polk for the Presidency in 1844, and also Cass in 1848, upon a platform which declared that "the Constitution did *not* confer authority upon the federal government, either directly or indirectly, to assume the debts of the several States," created for "State purposes." Thus it was fortunate for Texas that she confided her fortunes to the control of sympathizing friends, who enabled her to thrust her arms, figuratively, into the national treasury and extract therefrom $17,000,000, in reward of her fidelity to those friends—or, speaking with more exactness, permitting those friends to do so.

We have seen what arrangements were made by Polk himself—to which Jackson manifestly would never have consented if he had been consulted—to procure the support of the nullifiers of South Carolina and the electoral vote of that State. To the same spirit that prompted this combination, the country was indebted for the pretended and false claim to Oregon up to 54° and 40′ of north latitude. This nullification alliance was disguised by loud professions of devotion to the Union, and the Oregon claim was vociferously and constantly announced by these mottoes, printed upon flying banners: "All of Oregon or none"—"Fifty-four forty or fight." The popular vig-

ilance ought to have been sufficient to penetrate these
gauzy devices, yet it was not.   Instead, reason abdi-
cated her throne *to passion*, and by inflamed appeals to
national pride and eloquent dissertations upon our "manifest destiny," a popular verdict was rendered, seemingly
in approval of this demand.   The contest was one wherein
a question purely diplomatic was transferred by an *ex parte*
appeal to the patriotic impulses of the American people,to
a tribunal not recognized by the law of nations.   It involved great and intricate questions of international law,
the interpretation of treaties, agreements between the
United States and Great Britain, and a multitude of facts
connected with the discovery and former joint occupancy
of Oregon by both nations.   It had been discussed by
such British statesmen as Peel, Packenham, Aberdeen
and others, with some of our own most distinguished
men, such as Gallatin, John Quincy Adams and others,
and involved the question of title to the country which
not one voter out of ten thousand knew anything about
or possessed the means of impartial inquiry regarding it.
And it involved controversy with the most powerful nation in the world—a nation not likely to be intimidated
by mere bravado and foolish threats.   And yet the United
States were placed in the undignified attitude of submit-
ting this complicated question of law and fact to the people, to be decided at a popular election and under the
influence of intensified popular excitement.

   All this was done to contribute to the election of Polk,
and when that was accomplished by the threat that we
would have "all of Oregon or none," he became suddenly paralyzed when awakened to the actual reality that

Great Britain was not frightened at our bluster and was far better prepared for war than we were. Tyler had displayed more wisdom and discretion, for he offered to Great Britain to settle the long-continued controversy by fixing the boundary between Oregon and the British possessions at the 49th parallel of latitude. This, however, was then declined; and the bold and uncompromising demand for the line at 54° 40', in order to create a furor in favor of Polk and secure his election, incited the British authorities to put that country in a condition for war with the United States. But before avowing any actual readiness for hostilities, Great Britain renewed the proposition it had formerly rejected, and proposed the 49th parallel as the boundary. When this proposition reached Polk he must have been greatly embarrassed, for he could not have failed to know that its rejection meant war with Great Britain. The United States were not in a condition for such a war. The navy of that country greatly exceeded ours, and would have swept all our war vessels from the ocean. Our commerce would have been destroyed. Realizing all this, Polk was confronted by the pledge he and his supporters had made to the country, that they would have "*all* of Oregon or none." This was a sad dilemma,—one which, during the exciting canvass for the Presidency, had been overlooked. It was the condition into which those are apt to get who make promises without considering the means or consequences of fulfilling them. He and his friends had made the issue of peace or war with Great Britain, and he saw, after the excitement had subsided, that the rejection of the English proposition would produce the latter, at the cost of many millions of dollars to the United States and the sacrifice of hundreds, and perhaps thousands, of human lives. There was but one method of escape, which was to *back squarely down!* This he could not do openly and frankly by trusting to the magnanimity of the American people, for that requires a degree of courage which not many men possess. Instead of this, he resorted to indirection,—probably not with the view of misleading the country but to prevent his administration from total overthrow. He knew that a majority of the Senate favored the acceptance of the British offer to fix the line at the 49th parallel; and as the Constitution vested the treaty-making power in the President and Senate, he addressed a confidential communication to that body soliciting its advice,—knowing, beforehand, what it would be. The Senate did as he expected and advised the acceptance of the British proposition, and the treaty between the United States and Great Britain which fixes the boundary between the two countries along the 49th parallel of north latitude, was concluded by James Buchanan, our Secretary of State, and the British Minister at Washington City, June 15, 1846, ratified by the British government and by the Senate, and proclaimed August 5, 1846, by President Polk himself! And thus a strip of territory 5° 40' in width—or over 350 miles—which he had declared should never be surrendered, and for the defense of the title to which he claimed to have been specially elected, was given up to Great Britain without consideration, and the government of the United States was placed before all the leading nations of the world in the attitude of having set up a false claim, and the people of having approved it. And this was done in the very face of the fact that the country had been lashed into an almost frenzied condition of excitement at being told of the encroachment of the British government upon our national rights,—after thousands of voices had been made hoarse in eloquent defense of our right to 54° 40' of north latitude; —after "fifty-four forty or fight," and "all of Oregon or none," had been flung forth upon myriads of banners in all parts of the country, and British rapacity had been the subject of almost incessant denunciation from the nomination of Polk up to the time of his election! This simple statement of facts is sufficient of itself, without further comment.

All of the present generation who have the leisure and patience to investigate them, should be impressed with the absolute necessity of guarding well all the approaches to the ballot-box, in order that the public suffrage may not be contaminated by corrupt partisan influences and the general welfare may not become dependent upon the interests and personal ambitions of scheming and plotting politicians.

It was not only believed but predicted by many of our ablest statesmen that the annexation of Texas would lead to war between the United States and Mexico. The Mexican minister at Washington had, while the proposition was pending, notified our government that Mexico would so consider it, because that country had never recognized the independence of Texas. The fact was that after the battle of San Jacinto actual fighting between the two armies had ceased, but a state of war existed liable to renewal of the fighting whenever either party had men and money to carry it on. If Great Britain or some strong military power had been in the position of Mexico there would have been neither difficulty nor dispute about this proposition, for the annexation of revolted territory by a foreign power has always been recognized by international law as an act of war. Hence, by the recognized regulations which govern the intercourse of the great nations the President of the United States was not justified in violating this principle. Independently of this general principle, however, the boundary which separated Texas from Mexico while the former was a Mexican province was the Nueces river; nor does there seem to have been any alteration of this while that relation existed. Texas, therefore, when she acquired her independence, having no other defined western boundary, could acquire title only to what she occupied, and, as she did not occupy beyond the Nueces river, had no title west of it. Her *purpose* of ultimately extending her boundary to the Rio Grande conferred no title between these rivers, which was a strip of unoccupied and desert territory. Hence, the claim of Texas to the Rio Grande was invalid for three reasons: first, she never occupied the territory; second, her western boundary had never been extended beyond the Nueces, and third, her independence had never been recognized by Mexico. And to this might properly be added another—that a state of war between Mexico and her still existed.

While the question of annexation was pending we heard a great deal regarding the former ownership of

Texas by the United States; and a vast amount of elo-
quence was expended in talking about its *re*-annexation,
as if we had been unjustly deprived of it and were merely
reclaiming our own. This was simply *"ad captandum
populus,"* and did not possess the merit of being plausible
to any familiar with the facts. By our treaty with
Spain, February 22, 1819, that country ceded East and
West Florida to us, and, in return for this, the United
States ceded to Spain all of what was included in Texas.
The boundaries of our cession extended north from the
mouth of the Sabine river, along the western bank of
that river to the 32d degree of latitude, thence north to
Red river, thence along that river to the 23d degree of
west longitude from Washington City, thence north to the
Arkansas river, thence along that river to its source in
42d degree north latitude, and thence by that parallel of
latitude, to the South Sea or Pacific Ocean. This turned
out to be a high price to pay for Florida, but it was not
then so considered, inasmuch as it enabled the southern
boundary of the Union to be extended to the Gulf of
Mexico. But regardless of the value, we had no more
right to this territory, after the treaty of 1819 with Spain,
than if we never had laid claim to it. It was solemnly
conveyed by us to Spain, and when Mexico established
her independence, what we had ceded became hers, and
she held it under the guarantees of our treaty. And
when Texas revolted from her and obtained independence, she took title only to the extent of her Mexican boundary, because neither when the United States
owned the country, nor by the treaty conveying it to
Spain, nor by the Mexican law while she remained

a province of that country, was her western boundary
extended beyond the Nueces river. It must, consequently, be an accepted fact that, at the time of the
annexation to the United States, the western boundary
line of Texas was the Nueces river; and equally well accepted that the mere *ex parte* claim set up by Texas of
title to the Rio Grande river conferred no right, inasmuch as the two countries were at war, and Mexico both
denied and resisted it. Therefore, the administration of
Polk had no right, either by international or any other
law, to assume that the Rio Grande was the western
boundary of Texas, in the face of the existing war between Texas and Mexico, and to march our army to the
Rio Grande. On the contrary, it was an act of war towards Mexico, which, in self-defense, she was bound to resist or acquiesce in her own dismemberment and disgrace.
If Polk had been dealing with a strong instead of a weak
power—with Great Britain for example—he would not
have done so. Of this there is conclusive evidence in
the fact that he not only did not move our army up to
54° 40′ in Oregon to protect our title, but when he found
that strong power ready for war surrendered 5° 40′ of latitude, or over 300 miles of territory, in the very face of
his threat of "fifty-four forty or fight!" Now, however,
when the passions of that period have entirely subsided
and the number of those who remember how intensely
they burned is becoming fewer every day, it is proper to
inquire by what authority he moved the army of the
United States beyond our national boundary for *any* purpose, without the knowledge and consent of Congress.
The Constitution wisely gives to Congress alone the

power to declare war, and the President who assumes this prerogative violates both the Constitution and the spirit of our popular form of government. A careful inspection of the facts will show a series of flagrant executive acts of precisely this character, all manifestly intended to force Mexico into a war for the dismemberment of her territory and to gratify the war spirit he and his friends had aroused by their blustering claim to *all* of Oregon. The facts do not warrant any other conclusion.

The joint resolution for the annexation of Texas was approved by Tyler March 1, 1845, three days after which Polk became President. It did not undertake to define the territorial limits of Texas or its western boundary. On the contrary, it expressly provided as a primary condition that the State of Texas was to be thereafter "formed, subject to the adjustment by *this government* of *all questions of boundary* that may arise with other governments"—that is, with Mexico, the only other government interested. Let it be remembered that this was only the act of the United States, and not of Texas. It did not annex Texas, but provided for *future* annexation when she gave her consent in proper form. It was supposed she would do this, but she had not yet done it. Until she did our joint resolution was a mere offer to take her into our Union, which she could accept or reject as she pleased. In such matters nothing is taken by intendment. Consequently the resolution gave to the United States no authority or jurisdiction beyond the Sabine river which was the boundary of Texas upon the east, nor could any such authority or jurisdiction ex-

ist until the act of annexation became a consummated
fact by the consent of Texas. This consent was not
given until July 4, 1845, when the convention of Texas
agreed to the resolution of annexation, and consequently
upon that date, and not before, Texas became part of
the United States, and up till then the Sabine river was
our western boundary. Therefore, the United States
had nothing rightfully to do previous to that time with
the boundary between Texas and Mexico, but had proposed to Texas by the joint resolution providing for annexation, that when she became a part of our Union the
"government," not the President, would settle the question of boundary with Mexico, and Texas had assented
to annexation upon that express and primary condition.
Nevertheless—and this fact should be carefully noted—
on June 15, 1845, nineteen days *before* Texas had consented to annexation and at least twenty-five days before
the notification of her assent could have reached Washington as there was then no telegraph to Texas, Polk
caused to be sent from the War Department a "confidential" letter to General Z. Taylor, then at Fort Jessup,
commanding him to advance with the troops under his
command "to the mouth of the Sabine, or to such other
point on the Gulf of Mexico or its navigable waters as,
in your [*his*] judgment, may be found most convenient
for an embarkation at the proper time for *the western
frontier of Texas,*" and notifying him also that his "ultimate destination" was *"on or near the Rio Grande del
Norte."* This command had, of course, to be obeyed
by Taylor, who had no discretion in the matter. He
was instructed that the army of the United States had

for its ultimate destination a point beyond the territorial limits of the nation, which the President had no more constitutional power to order than he had to send it to the City of Mexico or to the Island of Cuba. Even if Texas had assented to the resolution of annexation the express terms were that the boundary between her and Mexico should be settled by *"the government"* with that country. It need not be said that the President is not "the government," although Polk seems to have supposed that *he* was when he undertook to substitute himself for it and to decide, *before* annexation was consummated, that the Rio Grande was the boundary between Texas and Mexico, and in order to maintain it as such prepared the army to be sent beyond the limits of the Union in order that it might be thereafter in a position to maintain the Rio Grande as that boundary. How differently he acted with Great Britain when the Oregon boundary was involved! Then he asked the Senate to come to his relief and advise him where the boundary should be, because Great Britain was a strong power. But in the case of the boundary between Texas and Mexico—a weak power —he chose to exercise the imperial prerogative right to decide it for himself, before Texas was part of the United States, and secretly and confidentially to order the army to be held in readiness for marching outside the territorial limits of the United States in order that it might be in readiness "at the proper time" to maintain that boundary against Mexico, although he knew beforehand, as well as he did afterward, that it would involve the United States in a foreign war. In all the history of this country nothing comparable to this has ever oc- .

18

curred—nothing so flagrantly violative of the National Constitution. For that reason, as well as others, the Congressional House of Representatives was fully justified in deciding, as it did, that the war with Mexico was brought on by the President in violation of the Constitution.

Taylor took possession of Corpus Christi, on the *west* side of the *Nueces* river, and near its mouth, in August, 1845—only four or five weeks after Texas had consented to annexation. When this became known it was pretended by the defenders of the administration that this movement of our army was in consequence of a request upon our government by Texas to resist the army of Mexico, inasmuch as that country had threatened retaliation in consequence of annexation. But when the facts became public, they clearly disproved this pretext; for, as has been stated, the original order to Taylor was dated at least nineteen days *before* Texas had assented to annexation, and while she was a foreign and independent State, and had, consequently, no right to ask the intervention of the United States; and if she had asked it, the President had no constitutional power to grant it. Having, however, obtained this position for our army, so that it could observe the movements of Mexico, the President sent a minister to Mexico in the person of John Slidell, under the additional pretense of settling the questions in dispute between the two countries. Slidell landed at Vera Cruz November 30, 1845, and, after full deliberation, the Mexican authorities notified him, March 1, 1846, that they would not treat with the United States, because they would not quietly

"suffer the nation to be despoiled of its territories"—
manifestly considering the army of Taylor as then occupying Mexican soil—that is, the territory between the
Nueces and the Rio Grande rivers, which was in dispute
between that country and Texas. The rejection of Slidell furnished an additional pretext for the friends of the
administration, which was that Mexico had offered an in-
dignity to the United States which justified the military
invasion of her territory. But this was an after thought
—not even plausible—for Polk had imperiously decided,
before Slidell was sent to Mexico, that the Rio Grande
was the western boundary of Texas, in direct violation of
the resolution of annexation, and, to prepare for enforc-
ing his decision, had sent Taylor with his army into the
disputed territory, in face of the fact that hostile relations existed between Texas and Mexico. More than
this, while Slidell was in Mexico, endeavoring to get himself recognized as Minister—that is, on January 13,
1846, Polk commanded Taylor to break up his camp at
Corpus Christi and advance to the Rio Grande.

From this it may be fairly presumed that Slidell was
employed to coquet with the Mexican authorities and
create a false sense of security in their minds, so that
while the United States was holding out the olive branch
of peace in one hand the other was secretly employed in
drawing the sword. Taylor had then been resting some
months at Corpus Christi awaiting instructions from those
upon whom rested all the responsibility for his movements. It was his duty to obey the orders of the President, his superior, and he accordingly moved his troops
forward to the Rio Grande, while Slidell was holding out

the false pretense to the Mexicans of desiring peace. There is something about this mission of Slidell which has never yet been exposed to public inspection; if it had been it might have thrown a flood of light upon what now seems to be a secret intrigue. It might show, and doubtless would, that this intrigue was carefully planned before he left the United States, in order to bring about what actually occurred, a war with Mexico and the acquisition by the United States of enough of her territory to stretch our possessions to the Pacific, and thus compensate for the loss of territory in Oregon which Polk and his friends, in every form of asseveration, claimed as ours. The House of Representatives in 1848 passed a resolution calling upon him for copies of "the instructions and orders" issued to Slidell before his departure for Mexico, supposing that the country had the legitimate right to know in what manner the administration, without the knowledge and consent of either Congress or the people, had involved us in a foreign war. But on January 12, 1848, Polk sent a message to the House wherein he informed that body that he declined a compliance with their request, considering it his "constitutional right" and "solemn duty, under the circumstances," not to let his instructions become public, because Mexico might thereby learn something that would prejudice the interests of the United States. Now, of course, when the principal parties are all dead, these secret instructions will never be exposed, but it will be difficult to persuade intelligent and impartial people of the present time that they were not discreditable to their authors. He pretended to justify his refusal upon the ground that it might prejudice future negotiations with Mexico for her to know what Slidell had been instructed, but this was not even an excuse, for the reason that war with Mexico then actually existed, and the country had the right to know whether it had been brought on by Mexico herself or by a combination of politicians who subordinated the interests and honor of the nation to their own ambition. All experience teaches that concealment is more frequently a badge of fraud than evidence of innocence.

During the march of Taylor to the Rio Grande he was several times notified by the Mexican authorities that his movement was regarded by Mexico as an act of war, but he had no discretion, as he was acting under orders from the President, and continued to advance until he reached Point Isabel on the coast and not very far from the Rio Grande. He soon obtained possession of the mouth of that river, where he erected defenses, and in a few days camped on its east bank opposite the Mexican city of Matamoras, upon the west bank. Here he constructed field-works and a strong fortress, which the Mexicans had the right to consider as a notification to them that he was ready to be attacked when they thought proper to do so. Instead of this, however, the Mexican general in command at Matamoras notified him that if he did not break up his camp he would be fired on. He refused, and returned for answer that the flag of the United States would continue to float where he had hoisted it. In a few days another division of the Mexican army arrived at Matamoras, when the commanding general informed Taylor, April 24, 1846, that " he considered hostilities commenced and should prosecute them." Up to this time no gun had been fired on either side. Taylor, on the same day, sent a detachment of sixty-three dragoons up the east bank of the Rio Grande to reconnoiter. On the next morning this detachment encountered two hundred Mexicans who had crossed over to that bank. Which first fired upon the other is not certain—each claiming to have been attacked. It is certain, however, that the warlike demonstrations which preceded their coming together indicated upon both sides a preparation for actual war and an intention to bring it on. It may properly be called a pitched battle for which both parties were in readiness. Taylor had built Fort Brown and planted his guns so that they bore upon the public square of Matamoras, and the Mexicans had made all the preparations for fighting in their power. And this was also certain, that Texas had never occupied the east bank of the Rio Grande, but the Mexicans had, and were then in possession of it. The country between there and the Neuces was a sterile desert, which had never been populated. Texas had no settlement west of the Neuces except Corpus Christi and its neighborhood, so that if she had even a shadow of right west of that river it did not extend to the Rio Grande, but left the strip of unoccupied territory—about three hundred miles wide—the true line of separation between her and Mexico. Not a single Texan had ever lived upon the Rio Grande, but only Mexicans. These two bodies of hostile forces were marching upon territory in possession of the Mexicans—

each having threatened to fire upon the other. Which fired first is of but little consequence, in point of fact, inasmuch as the battle they fought was the first of the Mexican war—its actual beginning. Sixteen of Taylor's dragoons were killed in the fight and the remainder were taken prisoners by the Mexicans; and this shedding of blood led to several years of terrible and desolating war. Before then nothing but paper bullets had been used—protests and counter-protests. But now a battle had been fought, blood had been shed, prisoners had been taken, and the "dogs of war" were turned loose. We must not, however, fight its battles over,—not even to express the exultation we all feel at the gallantry of our brave countrymen who bore the starry flag in triumph from Monterey to Buena Vista, and from Vera Cruz to the " Hall of Montezuma."

Immediately upon receiving intelligence of this skirmish upon the Rio Grande, for which both sides gradually and purposely prepared, the Presidential wrath was kindled to an excessive degree, because Polk saw in it the accomplishment of the object he sought after so anxiously—a war with Mexico. He and his friends had roused up the war spirit by threatening to take "all of Oregon" from Great Britain by force of arms, but as he had just decided to abate his haughty demand and *back down* at English threats, he manifestly hailed this intelligence with joy and delight—seeing in it, as he doubtless did, that the war spirit he had enkindled would then be gratified. He accordingly, on May 11, 1846, sent to Congress a war message, wherein he announced the actual existence of war—the plain meaning of which was that he had so managed as to bring on a war with Mexico independently of Congress, which was then in session, and to which alone the Constitution had given the power to declare war.   He had, before that time, carefully concealed from Congress and the country that he alone, and without the authority of law, had exercised the prerogative right to decide that the Rio Grande was the western boundary of Texas—in the face of the resolution of annexation, which provided that "the government should settle that question with Mexico after annexation, and had ordered Taylor to advance his troops beyond the Nueces with the ultimate purpose of going to that boundary and maintaining it by force of arms.   He neglected also to explain the fact that the skirmish in which the first blood was spilt, which he magnified into a battle, was prepared for by both armies in advance, and that it was fought upon ground which had never been in the possession of Texas, or even of a single Texan, but was then occupied by Mexicans alone.   Instead of these necessary and important explanations he represented that the Mexicans, by crossing the Rio Grande, had invaded the territory of the United States and "shed American blood upon American soil," in which representation "the wish was father to the thought."   And an obedient Congress, seemingly regardless of the obligation not to falsify the historic record, passed an act strangely preceded by a preamble which recited that, "whereas, by the act of the republic of Mexico a state of war exists between that government and the United States."   Why this cautiously worded recital?   A preamble is not necessary to a law, nor is it common to attach one to a law.   It serves only as an index to the meaning of a statute, furnishing a mere rule of interpretation. In this instance there was not the least necessity for it unless it was deemed necessary to explain something that needed explanation. From the fact that it was then used, the purpose to mislead might be legitimately inferred. A few words only were necessary to declare war constitutionally. But if this had been done the President would not have been relieved from the responsibility of having usurped the constitutional prerogative of "the government" to settle the western boundary of Texas with Mexico, and having ordered Taylor to march beyond the limits of the United States into territory in dispute between Mexico and Texas without authority of law and in violation of the Constitution. Hence the necessity for this preamble, which, being false, remains a blot upon the national statute-book, still continuing to mislead the unwary and all who, after nearly half a century has elapsed, have neither the leisure nor the means to discover the precise truth.

Besides the foregoing facts there are many others of like import found upon the records of the government, which combine to prove, and which do incontestibly prove, that Polk entered upon the Presidency with the fixed and resolute intention of forcing Mexico into a war for the purpose of taking from her such territory as he coveted by way of "indemnity," and that he prosecuted this purpose secretly until his ends were accomplished without consulting Congress, in violation of the Constitution. In addition to the objects he had in view, as already suggested, there was another, which to him undoubtedly was of controlling importance—that is, to ac-

quire Mexican territory upon the same parallels of latitude as the slave States, with the ultimate expectation of
seeing slavery introduced within those lines and by this
means increasing the political power of the South.   This
is evidenced by the fact that after the territory compos-
ing California and New Mexico had been acquired he ar-
gued, in his message of December 5, 1848, to prove
that each of them would have the constitutional right to
establish slavery or not at discretion, and that the doctrine which prohibited States formed north of the parallel of 36° 30' from becoming slave was not consistent
with the Constitution, but could be maintained only upon
the ground that it was the result of compromise.   It is
further attested by the additional fact that when the suspicion of his purpose in this respect approached almost
to positive knowledge, one who had supported him for the
Presidency introduced in Congress what became known
as the "Wilmot Proviso," which was intended to prevent
the introduction of slavery into any of the territory that
might be acquired from Mexico.   Whatever his intention, however, his reliance was mainly upon the united
South, against a divided North.   And believing that
with this strong support at his back he could defy all opposition, he executed his purposes with a strong hand, as
if he were an absolute monarch, instead of a constitutional President with limited and well defined powers.

Not only did he cause, beforehand, a large number of
war vessels to hover about the eastern coast of Mexico to await the state of war which he intended to
bring on, but he concentrated a large fleet in the Pacific,
along the Mexican coast line of California, for the same

purpose. What secret instructions he gave to the commanders of these fleets has not been discovered, but enough is known to show, beyond any reasonable doubt, that they were commanded, in advance, to take possession of and hold California as conquered territory, never to be surrendered, but to become part of the United States. The Pacific fleet was commanded by Commodore Sloat, who, as he says himself, had received instructions from the Secretary of the Navy dated June 24, 1846, by which he must have been instructed to do what he did,—for there was no officer of the navy who would have done so without peremptory instructions. The act of Congress declaring war to exist "by the act of Mexico" was approved May 13, 1846, so that these instructions must have been issued a little over one month after that time,—making it certain that the object to be accomplished, whatever it was, had been then decided upon. On July 7, 1846—with several war vessels under his command and others at San Francisco—Commodore Sloat demanded of the military commandant at Monterey in California, the unconditional surrender of everything in California under his "control and jurisdiction." Having accomplished this without bloodshed he, on the same day, issued from his flag-ship a proclamation "to the inhabitants of California," informing them that "*henceforth California will be a portion of the United States.*" He must be very credulous who supposes that this was done without special instructions from Washington. But there is more to the same import, which will remove all doubt upon that subject, if any should exist. He proceeded to tell them that they should have the same protection as

the citizens of "any other State in the Union,"—as if the
object he knew to be designed by the administration had
already been accomplished,—and that such as were not
disposed to accept the "privileges of citizenship, and to
live peaceably under the government of the United
States," would be "allowed to dispose of their property
and to remove quietly out of the country," or if they did
not, would be required to observe "strict neutrality."
In a general order issued the same day he declared it to
be his "duty to take California" and to "preserve it afterwards as a *part of the United States*, at all hazards."
With this object in view he demanded its surrender from
the commandant-general, and issued an order to Commander Montgomery,—then in command of the war-ship
Portsmouth at San Francisco—to "secure the bay of San
Francisco as soon as possible, at all events."   These objects were easily accomplished, as the Mexicans had
made no preparations for the military defense of San
Francisco, any more than Monterey, and in point of fact
did not generally know that actual war had broken out
between the United States and Mexico.   The possession
of these two important points was, therefore, obtained
without bloodshed or even resistance, and when this was
accomplished Commodore Sloat turned over the command of the conquering fleet to Commodore Stockton,
who, as subsequent events abundantly prove, must have
been as well instructed as he was, with regard to the purposes and policy of the administration.   It did not take
him long to discover that the Mexican population was
thrown into a condition of consternation and was very
much demoralized, and that the whole machinery of civil

government was, in a large measure, suspended. Under this condition of affairs the Mexican commandant-general of California sent to him a deputation of officers proposing to enter into negotiations with him, manifestly with the desire of adopting some regulations for protecting the rights of persons and property. He declined the proposition to negotiate, and proceeded immediately to organize a military expedition with the purpose of penetrating the interior of the 'country and take possession of it. This force met with no resistance, as the Mexicans fled before it, and on August 13, 1846, it took military possession of Los Angeles without firing a gun. The military commandant and the governor-in-chief of California thereupon fled from the territory, leaving this victorious army in possession of the entire power. Never was there before, in the history of the world, a more bloodless conquest, not having required the explosion of a single ounce of powder! The Mexicans were paralyzed, and fled in every direction whenever a body of armed men appeared.

As war had then existed between the two countries for about three months, California then became, by the custom of civilized nations, subject to martial law—government by military power. To such government it would undoubtedly have been subjected if Commodore Stockton had not been well informed—as Commodore Sloat had been—that it was the intention of the administration to seize upon California before the Mexicans could prepare for resistance, and to consider it, from the date of the capture of Monterey, as an integral part of the United States, without any reference whatever to the opinion

of Congress, or the will of the people. Consequently—
as Commodore Stockton says himself—he " forthwith de-
termined to organize a temporary *civil government*, to
conduct public affairs and to administer justice as in time
of peace." He could not wait for the action of Congress, but " forthwith " organized and established this
"civil government " over a country not yet a part of the
United States, and only a few days after he had expelled
a large number of its peaceable inhabitants with an armed
force! He then proceeded to construct what he called
the "frame of civil administration," by prescribing the
laws, creating courts, appointing judges and executive
officers, regulating " taxes and imposts " and prescribing appropriate punishments for offenses. And then he
—a commodore in the navy, without the least authority
of law, either civil or military—made himself the civil
governor over all! And when this was done he hastened
to exercise imperial powers by organizing the militia, appointing its officers, and creating military commandants
of Northern and Southern California. And when he
found it necessary to be absent he appointed an acting
governor *ad interim* in his place! And all this was done
under a government with a written Constitution and laws,
and under an administration whose Presidential chief
made it his proudest political boast that he was a strict
constructionist! At the time these occurrences took place
it was charged that they were directed by the administration and were necessary links in the chain of the executive policy of the government, and that the President
himself was not only cognizant of but actually directed
these violations of the Constitution. But this charge was

lustily denied until the policy of the administration was fulfilled by the treaty of Guadalupe Hidalgo—which ceded
California and New Mexico to the United States—when
all demands for inquiry into the truth were drowned by
shouts of exultation at the glorious destiny of the nation,
which had stretched itself out to the Pacific. When this
was accomplished and Mexico lay in humiliation at our
feet, Commodore Stockton deemed it necessary to his
own fame that he should explain with minuteness his
own personal agency in the work of conquest. Consequently, on February 18, 1848,—after the news had
reached the United States that the treaty of Guadalupe
Hidalgo had been agreed to—he laid before the Secretary of the Navy a full and detailed report of his proceedings in California; wherein, after enumerating the general facts of which he was cognizant, and especially his
institution of civil government, he says: "These acts
and intentions were *officially communicated to the department* in my official dispatches." And he declared his
gratification at knowing "how entirely I [he] had *anticipated the views of the government in the measures which
I* [he] *had adopted."*

Now, when so few of those who participated in these
events survive, their narration reads almost like romance—
bordering closely upon some of the tales of the Arabian
Nights. It must almost stagger the credulity of the
present generation to learn with what boldness and im-
punity the Constitution was violated in making war without the consent of Congress,—in waging it for the object
of violently wresting territory from a weak and neighbor-
ing nation,—in governing that territory when obtained

by civil institutions created by military power and maintained by bayonets,—and in studiously concealing all the important facts connected with these transactions upon the pretense that public interests would be prejudiced by their exposure.

When Lieutenant-General Scott marched victoriously with his gallant army from Vera Cruz to the city of Mexico and dismay seized upon the nation, the administration soon found itself in possession of sufficient power to dictate the terms of peace. Under the pretext of "indemnity" it demanded territory, the very territory it had brought on the war to acquire. And the consequence was that Mexico, humbled by defeat, entered into the treaty of Guadalupe Hidalgo, February 2, 1848, by which the boundary between the two countries was extended from the Rio Grande to the Pacific ocean, and, in consideration of the sum of $15,000,000, California and New Mexico were ceded to the United States. In the meantime, however, as already stated, one of the supporters of Polk, who suspected that the purpose of this acquisition of territory was to extend slavery and by this means weaken the political power of the North, introduced into Congress the "Wilmot Proviso," the express object of which was to prohibit the introduction of slavery into any of the territories of the United States. This was a political bombshell, heavily charged with the most inflammable materials. It excited both sections, but the South more than the North. There it aroused the most violent passions, and no man could gain the public favor who did not denounce the North for contemplated aggression upon the constitutional rights of the South, among which, as Polk and his administration maintained, was the right of the slaveholder to carry his slave property to the territories, and the right of the territories, upon coming into the Union, to establish slavery or not at their own discretion, any prohibitory statute of the United States to the contrary notwithstanding. But for the acquisition of Mexican territory these questions would have been of little practical import and slavery agitation would have ceased, like a fire which goes out for lack of kindling. That acquisition consequently was like the opening of Pandora's box—scattering evils of vast magnitude in every direction throughout the country. These were visited upon the South far more than upon the North, for there the multitude became so lashed into violent and consuming passion that reason was cast aside, so that when it became understood that the people of the United States were unwilling that the free territory they had obtained, however acquired, should be converted into slave States, the South inaugurated civil war against the Union, invited the destruction of its homes, the desolation of its fields, the sacrifice of the lives of its bravest sons and the destruction of slavery in the United States forever. What the South designed to protect it destroyed, and its bleeding wounds told the tale of the sad penalty it paid for its folly and madness.

He who reads history intelligently and comprehends its philosophy, can not fail to observe how the links fit together in the chain of events which lie between the annexation of Texas and the late civil war. The question of annexation nominated and elected Polk, and neither could have occurred without it; he, by violating the

19

Constitution, brought on the war with Mexico;—this led to the acquisition of foreign territory and invited the " Wilmot Proviso;"—and the South, infuriated to madness because unable to plant slavery in this acquired territory, made war upon the Union.   Each of these events dove-tail together in close and inseparable connection; and it is not too late for the popular investigation of them, in order that the people—who are theoretically and ought to be actually the source of power—may understand how much the security of the government and the stability of our institutions depend upon their vigilance.   It is said that " history repeats itself;"—but in order that there may be no repetition of the events here recorded, the popular mind should not become so deluded by partisan aims and professions as to forget that " eternal vigilance is the price of liberty."

In so far as I observed the personal characteristics of Polk, they impressed me with the belief that he possessed many commendable private virtues.   But it was never pretended, so far as I know, that he belonged to the class of men who, like Jackson and many others, link their friends to them by " hooks of steel."   In speaking of him I would " nothing extenuate, nor set down aught in malice," but simply content myself by recounting his public and official acts, and suggesting the motives which influenced him, in so far as my mind was impressed at the time of their occurrence.   Whatever may have been his private virtues, within that charmed circle where the formal ceremonies of official intercourse are thrown aside, these convictions have sunk deep into my mind and are matured by reflections extending beyond the average period of human life,—that he did not belong to the class of men from whom a President of the United States ought properly to be chosen,—that by his election the country was afflicted with a multitude of calamities, among the saddest in its history,—and that such must be the impartial verdict of all who intelligently scan the true history of his administration.

Z. Taylor—

CHAPTER XII

ZACHARY TAYLOR

THE instinctive sagacity which permeates the body of the American people is such that it is difficult to conceal from them the personal qualities of a President. The few who hold direct intercourse with him carry away from the ''White House'' favorable or unfavorable impressions, which are easily communicated to the masses, and these either attract or repel according to circumstances. It was unfortunate for Polk that in his associations with others he exhibited none of that mesmeric influence with which Jackson was so bountifully supplied by nature; and the consequence was that while his intense partisanship was distasteful to the adversaries of his administration, he was unable to acquire the full confidence of those who had elected him. This latter fact, however, was not attributable to this cause alone; but, in a large measure, to their discovery of the surreptitious manner in which he had combined with the nullifiers of South Carolina, who were more hostile to Jackson than to any other prominent public man, because of his uncalculating devotion to the Union. The ''old hero'' had died during the first year of Polk's administration—June 8, 1845—but, before his death, had so emphatically expressed his condemnation of the plot between Polk and

Tyler, whereby it was intended not only to sacrifice his friend Blair to the vengeance of the nullifiers, but to enable the latter to regain what they had lost in their controversy with him, that when the nominating convention met, May 22, 1848, it did not require a very vivid fancy to imagine that his spirit hovered over the body, in order so to guide and direct its proceedings as to prevent the renomination of Polk and add his name to the list of one-term Presidents. This was not difficult to do, for the rivalries and jealousies were so violent that harmony was impossible. The course of the administration with reference to the war with Mexico, and its unconcealed purpose to strengthen the slave power, had so disrupted the supporters of Polk in the great State of New York, that each faction of them had sent delegates to the convention, so widely separated with regard to these and kindred matters that when it was decided to admit both sets neither would consent to act, and the convention proceeded to nominate candidates without any representation from that State. The result was—as it was intended it should be—that *Polk did not receive a single vote!* General Lewis Cass of Michigan was nominated for President and General William O. Butler of Kentucky for Vice-President, and a platform was adopted rivaling in platitudes that of the Liberty party in 1843. A few words were added complimentary to Polk, which were intended to be the only reward he should be permitted to take with him into the retirement to which the convention very deliberately invited him!

The disaffection among the original supporters of Polk in New York soon began to bear unexpected fruits.

Taking to themselves the new and significant name of "Barn-burners," they assembled in convention at Utica, in that State, June 22, 1848—just one month after the nomination of Cass—and nominated Van Buren for the Presidency. This was intended to be preliminary, merely —like forming a skirmish-line preparatory to battle. The purpose of the movement was not long concealed, for on August 6, 1848, another convention, which included this same disaffected New York element, assembled at Buffalo, and was composed of delegates from every Northern State, and from Maryland, Virginia and the District of Columbia. This convention also nominated Van Buren for President, and along with him, Charles Francis Adams, of Massachusetts, for Vice-President, and adopted a platform expressly condemning and rebuking "the aggressions of the slave power," as indicated by the efforts then in progress to carry slavery into free territory. And that there should be no suspicion of the design to interfere with slavery in the States, this platform denied the power of Congress to do so, leaving that question to be decided by the States themselves. If there had been confusion before, it was "worse confounded" then. It had been fairly shown at the nominating convention of 1844 that Van Buren was the choice of the majority upon each of three ballotings, and was deprived of the nomination only by the cunningly contrived two-thirds rule, and contrary to the desire of Jackson, and it having been plainly discovered since then that his defeat and the election of Polk had led to the war with Mexico and the acquisition of free territory, those who composed this Buffalo convention considered it proper to nominate Van Buren in 1848, in order to keep the newly-acquired territory free, and to terminate the "aggressions of the slave power." They considered this to be mere retributive justice—more especially as the enemies of Van Buren, who had nominated and elected Polk, had, but a few weeks before, abandoned him entirely, without even the compliment of a single vote in the nominating convention.

National politics had, by this time, been brought into a tangled and confused state—so much so that, instead of looking to the deliberately-expressed public opinion as the guide of legislative proceedings, everything was submitted beforehand to the decision of party caucuses, whose decisions were held to be irreversible. He who conformed to them was held to be immaculate, while he who felt constrained by the force of his own convictions to oppose them was shunned and avoided as if he were a leper. The question of personal merit or demerit did not enter into the calculation, or, if it did, was subordinated to that which involved only the capacity for party services. Never before in the whole history of the government had this demoralizing doctrine received such positive executive approval as under the administrations of Van Buren, Tyler and Polk, each one of whom seemed to think that, whatever else befell the country, the system of official "rewards and punishments" must, at all events, be maintained. To the great bulk of the people, of all parties, this was an abhorrent practice, to which they were unwilling to become reconciled, because they saw in it only that which, if persisted in, would inevitably tend to convert the government into a mere party machine, to be used solely for sinister and selfish purposes, entirely regardless of the general welfare. To put an end to this tendency toward demoralization, the people, of all parties and sections, were constrained by the condition of affairs, which it was easy for them to trace to Polk's administration, to pause and consider whether or no they possessed a remedy they could efficiently apply, or whether their legitimate power had become so enfeebled by party machinations as to seriously threaten the longer existence of the right of self-government. The sentiment thus aroused was not entirely sectional, while—from causes heretofore stated—it existed more extensively in the North than in the South—there were, in the latter section, murmurings of disapprobation at the tendency to disunion, which, as they could easily see, had been produced by permitting the autocratic leaders of Southern opinion to exercise the prerogative right to form and mold it to suit themselves. The desire, therefore to arrest the downward tendency of national affairs, was participated in by multitudes of people in all the sections, and it is proper to consider it as having been eminently patriotic.

We have seen that Polk was laid aside and Cass nominated for the Presidency by a convention held May 22, 1848, upon a platform intensely partisan—an absolute notification to the country that, although the convention was unwilling to trust Polk a second term, its purpose was, if successful with another candidate, to conduct the government consistently with the policy of his administration as regarded both domestic and foreign affairs.

The people, irrespective of former parties, availed themselves of this notice to bring about another nominating
convention for the selection of an opposing candidate,
who should not be tied down by party bandages, but
should, if elected, so administer the government consistently with the Constitution as to advance the general
welfare and hold the bonds of Union inviolate. This
convention was composed of delegates from all the States,
united in the desire to prevent discord between the sections and harmonize elements which had been placed in
seeming, though not in actual, conflict by partisan excesses and sectional exactions. There were 280 delegates, which made it necessary that the nominee should
receive at least 141 votes, inasmuch as it was impossible
to form any such partisan and sectional combination as
that which had introduced the two-thirds rule eight years
before to defeat Van Buren. Two of the candidates
voted for were Clay and Webster, who were considered
as distinctively the representatives of party, but neither
of the other two, Generals Scott and Taylor, were looked
upon in that light, as they were both officers of the army
and had never been identified with partisan politics. It
was evident from the beginning that the main object of the
majority was to unite upon some man of this latter class
in order to give the people a fair opportunity to decide
whether or no they desired the government to be conducted in obedience to mere party dictation or for the
general welfare of all the sections. Taylor had agreed
to accept the nomination if tendered to him, but was unwilling to do anything that would contribute to that result. In his letter to Allison, written about five weeks

before, he had distinctly expressed his own "distrust" of
his "fitness" for a station so high as that of President,
and declared that he would "most gladly" retire from
the position of a candidate when his friends should manifest that wish.   In this letter, however, he went further
and touched a cord which led directly to the hearts of
those who desired to see the government lifted out of the
party grooves into which it had been plunged by Van
Buren, Tyler and Polk, and to place it again upon the
plane where the Revolutionary Presidents had left it.   In
enumerating the "cardinal principles" which he declared
would govern him if President, he said: "I am not sufficiently familiar with all the minute details of political
legislation to give solemn pledges to exert myself to carry
out this or defeat that measure," an exhibition of unpre-
tentious modesty which commended itself to all except
the politicians, who looked upon the people as qualified
only for the duty of obedience.

He proceeded, however, to say: "If elected, I would
not be the mere President of a party.   I would endeavor
to act independent of party domination.   I should feel
bound to administer the government untrammeled by
party schemes."   With reference to the veto power he
expressed some great and fundamental truths which
ought to remain deeply imbedded in the hearts and
minds of the people, when he said, "I have thought that
for many years past the known opinions and wishes of
the executive have exercised an undue and injurious influence upon the legislative department of the government; and for this cause I have thought our system was
in danger of undergoing a great change from its true the-

ory. *The personal opinions of the individual who may
happen to occupy the executive chair ought not to control
the action of Congress upon questions of domestic policy;*
nor ought his objections to be interposed where questions
of constitutional power have been settled by the various
departments of the government, and acquiesced in by the
people." Regarding measures of domestic policy—such
as "the tariff, the currency, the improvement of our
great highways, rivers, lakes and harbors," in his opinion, "the will of the people as expressed through their
representatives in Congress ought to be respected and
carried out by the Executive;"—in other words, he considered the people as possessing the governing power.
He added his congratulations upon the close of the Mexican war, and expressed the opinion that the principles
and true policy of the government were "opposed to the
subjugation of other nations and the dismemberment of
other countries by conquest." These truly conservative
and patriotic opinions not only arrested public attention
in every section of the Union, but so influenced the action of the convention that he was nominated for President on the fourth ballot; after which Millard Fillmore
of New York was nominated for Vice-President. Repeated efforts were thereupon made by a few to commit
the convention to a partisan contest, but they were inef-
fectual; and it adjourned without promulgating a party
platform—preferring to stand upon the foregoing plain
avowals of Taylor, and leaving his patriotism and merits
without any other voucher than was furnished by his
whole life-work.

The result of the election was somewhat disappointing,

although not disheartening to the truly conservative people throughout the United States. Taylor received 1,360,-101 of the popular vote, against 1,220,544 given to Cass, making his plurality over the latter 149,557. Van Buren, however, received 291,263 votes, which, if added to the vote of Cass, left Taylor in a minority of 141,706 of the whole popular vote. Taylor received majorities in fifteen States—eight free and seven slave; whereas, Cass received majorities in fourteen—eight free and six slave —South Carolina voting by the Legislature. The majorities for Taylor in the free States aggregated 141,865, against 53,685 for Cass; and in the slave States 42,295, against 18,226 for Cass; while Van Buren did not get a majority in a single State, although he received 6,192 votes in New York more than Cass, which caused Taylor to carry that State only by a plurality of 98,093 votes. This condition of things necessarily controlled the electoral vote, so that when cast Taylor and Fillmore received 163 each, and Cass and Butler 127 each,—the majorities of the two former being 46 electoral votes. And thus again—as had been the case when Polk was elected—the peculiar working of our Presidential elective system was practically exhibited. Nevertheless, the election had one aspect important enough to be remembered, as showing the condition of public opinion at that time, with reference to the sectional controversy into which Polk's administration had conducted the country. It is this: That the 98,180 votes received by Taylor over the majorities of Cass in the free States, and his excess of majorities of 24,069 over Cass in the slave States, demonstrated, beyond any doubt, that the people of both sections were tired of the strife which the partisan politicians had fomented, and that but for the subsequent renewal of this strife our disastrous civil war would have been escaped.

Taylor was not a great man, in the sense in which that term is commonly applied to American statesmen. But he was a man of clear, discriminating, and accurate judgment with regard to men and measures. His views of public policy were eminently conservative, inasmuch as both observation and experience had taught him that the government, instead of being experimented with in the interest of any political party, should be conducted as nearly as possible within the lines of a policy indicated by the examples of its founders. His life had been spent in the military service—in the camp and field—where, like a true soldier, he had acquired that patriotic love of country which kept his mind at a steady poise upon all subjects which regarded its domestic policy. His integrity of purpose was acknowledged to be of that sterling quality which is firmly and deeply rooted in the mind and governs all its impulses. He was, in fact, just such a man as the times demanded, to bring the government back into the paths marked out by " the fathers," and from which it had been led by scheming politicians, who measured it by no higher standard of value than as it contributed to their own successes. The popular mind was directed to him by his eminent services in the war with Mexico, where his skill as a commander had been so conspicuously displayed as to excite universal admiration. His selection as a candidate was made, therefore, more on account of his distinguishing virtues than the belief that he could ever become the participator in party or sectional strife. In so far as the Northern people were involved it was an offer of ''the olive branch of peace '' to the South,—for as he had been all his life identified with the institution of slavery, and had been accustomed to defend all the Constitutional rights of the slave States, there was no rational ground for believing that sectional animosity would receive the least encouragement from him or from others subject to his control. Many of the Southern people saw this, and were patriotic enough to vote accordingly; for he received popular majorities and the electoral votes of the following seven slave States: Florida, Georgia, Kentucky, Louisiana, Maryland, North Carolina, and Tennessee; while Cass received popular majorities in the remaining slave States, and the electoral vote of all of them, including South Carolina. Whether we call the sentiment thus encouraged conservative or by some other name, it was manifestly patriotic, and if it had grown as Taylor desired it to grow, the peace of the Union would not have been disturbed. Subsequent events proved, however, that the factionists did not intend this.

In his inaugural address he expressed his views of domestic policy so plainly and distinctly that they could not be misunderstood. Fully realizing the condition of the country, seriously threatened with the terrible consequences of sectional strife, he avowed his determination to ''defer with reverence'' to the ''illustrious patriots'' of the Revolutionary era,'' ''and especially to his example, who was, by so many titles, the 'Father of the Country,' '' and referring to various public interests which

would command his official attention and become the subjects of his executive recommendations, he said: "But
it is for the wisdom of Congress itself, in which all legislative powers are vested by the Constitution, to regulate
these and other matters of domestic policy," thus showing his confidence in our form of popular government
and in the capacity of the people to select their own representative agents.   It was not a suitable occasion for
any other than a mere reference to public questions, but
so intense was his devotion to the Union that he could
not refrain from invoking for it the "protecting care" of
Divine Providence, so that all "bitterness" between the
sections should be assuaged, "just and liberal principles"
be promulgated and that the public mind should be filled
with "an enlarged patriotism, which shall acknowledge
no limits but those of our own wide-spread republic."
There was not one who heard him but was impressed by
his candor, sincerity and patriotism.

Taylor was confronted at the beginning of his administration, March 4, 1849, by the condition of affairs in the
newly acquired territories, as left by Polk.   It came to
him as an official inheritance, which required in its management the extremest prudence and caution.   He had
never been a politician in the popular sense, but was careful to surround himself with a cabinet of counselors so
distinguished by true conservatism and ability that they
suffer nothing by comparison with their predecessors or
successors.   These were John M. Clayton, of Delaware,
Secretary of State; William M. Meredith, of Pennsylvania, Secretary of the Treasury; George W. Crawford, of
Georgia, Secretary of War; William B. Preston, of Vir-

ginia, Secretary of the Navy; Thomas Ewing, of Ohio, Secretary of the Interior; Jacob Collamer, of Vermont, Postmaster-General, and Reverdy Johnson, of Maryland, Attorney-General. From a President and cabinet thus constituted the country expected nothing else than what the public interest and honor required. Hence, there was no surprise when Taylor decided that it was his imperative duty to leave California and New Mexico precisely as he had found them—that is, in the position they occupied at the close of Polk's administration. To have done otherwise would have involved him in the necessity of either permitting the civil governments existing in those territories to be changed at the will of their inhabitants, or to prescribe such changes as seemed right to himself. Consistently with what he regarded as due to the nation, he could do neither, for the reason that as they had been created and were administered without authority of law it was his plain duty to omit doing anything that would show, or tend to show, that his executive approval was given to these illegal proceedings. Therefore, he awaited the assembling of Congress in December, 1850, and in his message called attention to the real condition of affairs and submitted to the legislative department, where the Constitution places it, the necessity of providing by law such forms of civil government for California and New Mexico as would prepare them for admission into the Union as States whenever they were fitted for that relation. By this method he thought the errors of the past might be escaped and "all causes of uneasiness" be avoided in the future. But he was too well aware of the sectional antagonism which the madness of faction had

20

created between portions of the Northern and Southern people, not to realize his obligation to express himself fully and plainly with regard to these proposed governments. How clearly he did this will be seen by the following extract from this message: "With a view of maintaining the harmony and tranquillity so dear to us all, we should abstain from the introduction of those exciting topics of a sectional character which have hitherto produced painful apprehensions in the public mind, and I repeat the solemn warning of the first and most illustrious of my predecessors against furnishing 'any ground for characterizing parties by geographical discriminations.'"

Herein Taylor displayed both wisdom and discretion. Knowing, as he did, the extent to which sectional prejudices had been invoked by the rival factions both North and South, and foreseeing the consequences to which they were likely to lead unless restrained, he regarded it his duty to rebuke the spirit of discord before it acquired vigor enough to imperil the Union. He did this by occupying ground between the two extremes—endeavoring, like a skillful navigator, to steer the ship of state between Scylla and Charybdis. To his prudent and thoughtful mind it was clear that the North was not prepared to consent to any system of national policy that would result in the creation of a slave State by national authority, and equally clear that the South would not consent to the "Wilmot Proviso," which was regarded in that section as the inauguration of a direct war against the equality of the States under the Constitution. Therefore, with the hope of producing reconciliation between the sections, he foreshadowed the safe and practical theory that when the people of California and New Mexico were called upon to form State Constitutions, they should be permitted, without any interference by Congress, to settle the question of slavery for themselves, and be admitted into the Union either as free or slave States, as they should decide. He fully realized the difficulties of the problem to be solved, but, realizing that the Union had been formed by the alliance of free and slave States, and that the Constitution had guaranteed to each the absolute right of government by their own laws, he could do nothing more than this, and to have done less would have required him to abandon his national position as President and identify himself with one or the other of the sections. To revive now the arguments by which his recommendation was resisted would be a fruitless task, inasmuch as there never can hereafter be an occasion for their repetition. It is proper to say, however, that the extreme Southern men in the Senate met the recommendation of Taylor by demanding, under the leadership of Jefferson Davis, that the Missouri Compromise line should be extended to the Pacific, and that there should be "the specific recognition of the right to hold slaves in the territory below that line, and that before such Territories are admitted into the Union as States, slaves may be taken there from any of the United States, at the option of the owners." To this it was replied by Clay, himself the owner of slaves and Senator from a slave State, that as the territory acquired from Mexico was free at the time it was ceded to the United States, he would never vote to make it slave.

In eloquent words which I have not forgotten—for I was present and heard him—he said: "Coming from a slave State, as I do, I owe it to myself, I owe it to truth, I owe it to the subject, to state that no earthly power could induce me to vote for a specific measure for the introduction of slavery where it had not before existed, either north or south of the" Missouri Compromise line. And thus the issue was so distinctly made up that the Senate deemed it expedient to appoint by ballot a committee of thirteen, to whom the subject of slavery in all its aspects should be referred, with a view to discover, if possible, some ground of compromise between the sections.

Clay was made chairman of this committee, and the remaining twelve were equally divided between the sections—the representatives of slavery being in the majority, consisting of the following Senators: Clay of Kentucky, Bell of Tennessee, Berrien of Georgia, Downs of Louisiana, King of Alabama, Mangum of North Carolina, and Mason of Virginia. The six Northern Senators were Dickinson of New York, Phelps of Vermont, Cass of Michigan, Webster of Massachusetts, Cooper of Pennsylvania, and Bright of Indiana. To such a committee—having upon it some of the foremost men of the nation—any important public question might well have been entrusted. Their deliberations continued more than two weeks, when, on May 8, 1850, Clay as chairman made a report with the following recommendations: *First*, That the division of Texas into new States be deferred; *second*, that California be forthwith admitted into the Union; *third*, that the "Wilmot Proviso" should not be applied to new Territories to be formed out of the territory acquired from Mexico; *fourth*, that the fugitive slave law should be more effectively executed between the States; *fifth*, that slavery where it existed should not be abolished; and *sixth*, that the slave-trade in the District of Columbia should be prohibited "under a heavy penalty." These propositions were embodied in several bills which gave rise to animated discussions in both Houses, but were passed into laws during that session of Congress. They constitute what has been called "the Clay compromise of 1850." It is not necessary to the fame of Taylor, however, to claim that this result was brought about, in any special degree, by his executive influence. All he did was to communicate his views to Congress and leave the Senate and House of Representatives to their own responsibilities. Nevertheless, if he had lived he would have had the satisfaction of realizing that his efforts to harmonize the sections were not unavailing, although the extreme men of the South were not reconciled. Of these latter there were eighteen in the Senate and fifty-six in the House who voted against the admission of California into the Union, because the people there had prohibited slavery. But for these, and others influenced by them, the questions pertaining to slavery would have been justly and amicably settled according to the policy of Taylor's administration. And his genuine conservatism—founded upon the obligation of obedience to the Constitution and the laws—would have been so diffused throughout the Union, among all classes, that the peaceful progress of the country could have been arrested only by departing from his example and disobeying his counsel. But just as the clouds were beginning to show their "silver lining" and the storm to abate, his career was suddenly arrested by the hand of death. Upon July 4, 1850, he was taken suddenly ill, and five days thereafter was a corpse in the executive mansion, His naturally strong and vigorous constitution had been so enfeebled by exposure and hard labor that it was unable to resist an attack so violent. But his courage was unfaltering to the last—that courage which makes the death of a departing Christian seem like a gentle slumber. These were his expiring words: *"I am ready to die. I have faithfully endeavored to do my duty."*

I never saw Taylor until the day of his inauguration, when I was most favorably impressed by his manner. He was without the least ostentation, and it was impossible to listen to what he said without feeling assured of his candor and sincerity. I once conversed with him with reference to the condition and course of public affairs, and have not forgotten the unlimited confidence he expressed in the capacity of the people to arrest the progress of wrong and error, when made conscious of their existence. Referring to the existing evidences of alienation between the North and the South, he gave it as his belief that if the people of both sections would take the matter in their own hands, independently of the politicians, such a condition of quiet and pacification would be brought about as would assure the stability of the Union. Upon this subject he expressed himself with great earnestness and zeal, and was most emphatic in declaring that, in his opinion, the country had been so misled by unduly excited passion as to have departed too far from the counsel of the wise men who constructed the government. That he was sincere in this was shown by the whole course of his short administration, which was characterized throughout by devotion to the teachings of "the Fathers." That it would have been so continued to the end of his constitutional term he solemnly pledged himself in these closing words of his only message to Congress—his last will and testament to the country: "But attachment to the Union of the States should be habitually fostered in every American heart. For more than half a century, during which kingdoms and empires have fallen, this Union has stood unshaken. The patriots who formed it have long since descended to the grave; yet still it remains the proudest monument to their memory, and the object of affection and admiration with every one worthy to bear the American name. In my judgment, its dissolution would be the greatest of calamities; and to avert that should be the study of every American. Upon its preservation must depend our happiness and that of countless generations to come. Whatever dangers may threaten it, *I shall stand by it and maintain it, in its integrity, to the full extent of the obligations imposed, and the power conferred upon me by the Constitution.*"

Millard Fillmore

CHAPTER XIII

MILLARD FILLMORE

My first acquaintance with Fillmore was formed at the extra session of Congress, called by President Harrison for May 31, 1841, in consequence of the financial embarrassment existing and the general derangement of business affairs throughout the country. By general consent he was made chairman of the committee of ways and means in the House of Representatives, which position he occupied during that entire Congress. Thus he became the leader of the House, for which he possessed the very highest qualifications. He was cool, calm and dispassionate and never suffered himself to become unduly excited, no matter how intensely the passions of party raged around him. I have met with few men who kept themselves at steadier equipoise. On this account the utmost attention was always paid to what he said, which commanded the respect even of those who disagreed with him. He never wasted words nor arraigned the motives of others, but in a thoroughly business-like manner confined himself to the immediate subject under consideration.

The bills which subsequently became the tariff law of 1842 were prepared under his auspices, and during the discussion of the first of these, which was vetoed by Tyler, the defense of the measure, in all its details and bearings, was confided to him. His mind was fully imbued with the principles embodied in the policy of protection, and these he defended upon every suitable occasion with conspicuous ability. He never endeavored to rival some of the opponents of that principle in animated and impassioned oratory, for in this particular field he was surpassed by several of them, but it was a common thing to see their fine-spun theories exploded by his powerful and faultless logic. His style of oratory was wholly unlike that of Wise, who was fiery and brilliant and often erratic, while he was always cool and collected and never impetuous. In the place of what Tacitus called "the thunder and lightning of oratory," his style was characterized by mathematical directness, and if he did not always convince he left no wound to rankle in the minds of his antagonists. He was, therefore, not merely a popular but a successful leader of the House, and came up to the full measure of responsibility which his position imposed upon him. I remember no instance to the contrary, although such a multitude of stirring events have been crowded into the intervening years as are well calculated to erase impressions which might otherwise have remained enduring.

When Fillmore became President by the death of Taylor, there was much speculation as to the course he would probably pursue with regard to the compromise measures then pending in Congress. It was supposed by some that, as a Northern man, and the former representative of a Northern constituency, his administration would tend to encourage sectionalism, if it did not become distinctively anti-slavery upon all measures then, or likely to be, proposed. On the other hand, those who knew him well and were familiar with his modes of thought were convinced that whatever course he deemed it his duty to pursue would be the result of calm deliberation and honest convictions. The former were disappointed, but the latter were not—for each of the compromise measures, in the order in which they were passed, became the law by his approval. In this respect he acted in precise conformity to the line of policy which Taylor had indicated, so that in so far as the slavery question was involved, the two administrations were in full accord. That he thereby caused some dissatisfaction in the North is undoubtedly true, but this came from the ''Barn-burners,'' as they were called, who had rallied to the support of Van Buren, and who, while they did not receive the popular vote of a single State, kept up their organization, well knowing that it had a two-fold effect—to divide the North and solidify the South. This, however, did not drive him from his course, and at this point in his history he exhibited, as it has always seemed to me, the very highest and most commendable qualities of statesmanship. He was no longer the representative of a local constituency in the North, and was not restrained in his official action alone by their desires nor bound by their instructions. He had become the President of the United States— not of any particular portion of the people, but of all. He was bound by the most solemn obligation to disregard all sectional interests, and to keep the Union welded together by the support of such measures as would lead to national harmony. Occupying this attitude,

he was confronted by a grave question of political ethics
—whether a President could rightfully set up his own
personal will against that of the nation, expressed in the
only form known to the Constitution—that is, whether it
was proper for him to interpose the executive *veto* to defeat any one of the compromise measures, inasmuch as
they involved expediency alone. His mind was trained
in a school wherein it has been taught that the most
essential fundamental principle of popular institutions is
the right of the people so to regulate the affairs of government as shall most conduce to the protection and ad-
vancement of their common welfare, in all matters not forbidden by the Constitution. And as it was not contend-
ed by any whose opinions were worthy of note that any
of the compromise measures were violative of the Constitution, his official duty was plain and simple. Hence,
the missiles aimed at him by Northern factionists were
harmless. They inflicted no wound upon his reputation,
nor did they in the least abate his ardor in the pursuit of
his official duties, as his conscience dictated them.

That which incited the most violent and vindictive
abuse of Fillmore, upon the part of those who boisterous-
ly invoked the spirit of sectionalism in the North, was his
approval of that part of the compromise which provided
for the more faithful execution of the fugitive slave law.
Every piece of artillery which belonged to the camp of
his adversaries was brought into action against him and
his administration, because, by this act, it was alleged
he had violated a principle of the natural law so flagrantly that he could not be forgiven. Every arrow aimed at
him had poison upon its point. They who engaged in

this work were designated as fanatics—and they were not misnamed. They were misled by their infuriated passions, and, by giving free indulgence to these, became the auxiliaries of the nullifiers in the South, as the nullifiers were their auxiliaries in the North. The one insisted that the Union should not stand unless slavery were abolished; the other that it should not unless slavery became triumphant over all opposition. The compromise measures were intended to rebuke both these factions, and therefore they were accepted, both North and South, as a truce between the sections. And innumerable facts have since occurred to prove that this compromise ought never to have been violated.

In approving the whole series of compromise measures Fillmore was governed by precedents he could not disregard without seriously endangering the public peace. His refusal to do so would have added fresh fuel to the flames which had been furiously burning but were then dying out. While his action was calculated to inspire renewed confidence in the strength and stability of the Union, it was at the same time a rebuke to those, both North and South, who had made the national interests secondary to their own by stirring up sectional prejudices and animosity. He realized that as truth is frequently found midway between the extremes of error, so the only true course of national safety lay midway between these sectional extremes. And he was convinced, moreover, that as the nation had been built up by concessions and compromises, it could be maintained and preserved only by cultivating and preserving the same spirit. The admission of California into the Union with a constitution

prohibiting slavery could not have occasioned any difficulty, in his mind, not only because that doctrine met the
popular approval in the election of Taylor and himself,
but because it accorded with his own personal opinion.
But the provision for the better enforcement of the fugitive slave law may have caused him to hesitate somewhat, inasmuch as that law had become specially odious
to a number of Northern people, who had not only refused to aid themselves, but insisted upon the enactment
of "personal liberty" laws and other measures whereby
others should be prohibited from aiding in its execution.
But he raised himself above the mere standard of the politician to that of the statesman.   In this he was inspired,
not only by his own patriotism, but by the example of all
his predecessors, including Washington, under whose administration the first fugitive slave law was enacted.   If
he had done otherwise he would have placed himself and
his administration in direct and palpable conflict with one
of the plainest provisions of the Constitution.   In that
national covenant it is provided that "no person held to
service or labor in one State, under the laws thereof, escaping into another, shall, in consequence of any law
or regulation therein, be discharged from such service or
labor, but shall be delivered up on claim of the party to
whom such service or labor may be due."   This did not
introduce slavery, but merely recognized the indisputable
fact that it existed.   Everybody in that day knew how
hard several of the slave States, during the colonial period, had struggled to put a stop to the slave trade, but
unavailingly.   It was equally well known also that immense sums of money had been invested in slave prop-

erty, but sudden emancipation, without compensation,
would reduce multitudes of people to bankruptcy; that
if the government were so inclined it would not possess the
means to provide compensation for the emancipated
slaves, and that no people ever lived, in ancient or modern times, who were willing or could afford to surrender
up so large an amount of wealth solely for the public
good. Consequently there was nothing more absolutely
and palpably demonstrated to the framers of the government than this—that unless the Constitution were formed
by the mutual assent of both free and slave States it could
not be formed at all, but the country would be left at the
mercy of Great Britain, or a prey to any combination of
monarchs who should resolve to put an end to popular
self-government, as the "allied powers" afterwards did at
the Congresses of Vienna and Verona.

There had never been any serious question about the
obligation which the Constitution had imposed upon Congress to enact a fugitive slave law so effective in its provisions that slaves escaping into the free States might be
reclaimed by their owners. But the difficulty lay in the
execution of the law—especially after the slavery agitation which followed the annexation of Texas. Among
the opponents of slavery in the North, there were some
who maintained that inasmuch as the divine law, in their
opinion, forbade the practice of holding a human being
in bondage, it was consequently sinful to arrest fugitive
slaves. If they had stopped at this mere expression of
belief, no practically injurious consequences would have
been likely to follow, for in that event they would have
left the law to be executed by those entrusted with that

duty. But they went further and insisted not only that
their consciences would not permit them to aid in the execution of the law, but required them to interfere actively
and prevent its execution by the public officers; in other
words, to resist the law of Congress. With this view
they procured as many laws to be enacted in the Northern States as they could, behind which they endeavored
to shield themselves from the consequences of violating
the national law; in this respect imitating the nullifiers
of the South by carrying the doctrine of State rights so
far as to justify resistance to the national authority.
With reference to the Constitution they called it "a covenant with hell," because it authorized the recapture of
fugitive slaves, and insisted upon the fundamental right
of each individual to set up in his own conscience a
"higher law" by which he could release himself from
the obligation of obedience to it. With this class of men
all enactments of Congress were invalid and without force
unless they corresponded with their own private and personal convictions of right, and Fillmore gave but little
consideration to their ravings, because he could easily
see that their success would both dissolve the Union and
produce general anarchy throughout the country. It is
not saying too much in his behalf to assert that in this he
exhibited wise and prudent statesmanship,—such as enables a President to disregard the demands of faction and
devote himself to the "general welfare" of the entire nation. If he had done nothing else while President but
approve the compromise measures of 1850, he would
have been entitled to the public thanks; for at a time
like that, when the national sky was darkened by threat-

ening clouds, it required true courage to defy the exasperated sectional factions then warring against the Constitution. Like Washington when he demanded the recall of the French minister Genet for plotting against the stability of the government, and Jackson when he struck nullification a paralyzing blow, he firmly resolved to stand by the national cause, to ''sink or swim, survive or perish'' with the Union.

Animated by the hope of future concord between the sections, Fillmore pledged his administration from the beginning to the maintenance of the compromise. This pledge involved nothing of party, but rose above it into a higher and better atmosphere, such as assured a strong and vigorous growth to the bonds of Union between all the States, both free and slave—that is, the Union as ''the fathers'' formed it. Hence, we find him, in his message of December 2, 1851, more than a year after the compromise measures were adopted, employing these inspiring words: ''The agitation which for a time threatened to disturb the fraternal relations which make us one people is fast subsiding, and a year of general prosperity and health has crowned the nation with unusual blessing. None can look back to the dangers which are passed, or forward to the bright prospects before us, without feeling a thrill of gratification, at the same time that he must be impressed with a grateful sense of our profound obligations to a beneficent Providence, whose paternal care is so manifest in the happiness of this highly-favored land.'' And—referring to what he had said in his message the year before, that he considered the compromise measures ''as a final set-

21

tlement" of all the perplexing questions involved—he again recommended strict "adherence to the adjustments established by those measures," and added: "Wide differences and jarring opinions can only be reconciled by yielding something on all sides, and this result had been reached after an angry conflict of many months, in which one part of the country was arrayed against another, and violent convulsion seemed to be imminent. Looking at the interests of the whole country, I felt it to be my duty to seize upon this compromise as the best that could be obtained amid conflicting interests, and to insist upon it as a final settlement, to be adhered to by all who value the peace and welfare of the country." From this it may be seen under what a strong sense of obligation to the nation he acted, and how steadily and courageously he pursued the line of constitutional duty. If he had interposed his executive *veto*—which enraged zealots urged him to do, with terrible threatenings in case of refusal —the country might have been then carried to the verge of that abyss above which it was suspended for several painful years, when, after his counsel was disregarded, the spirit of these compromise measures was unwisely violated. This, however, will be more distinctly realized hereafter, when it shall become necessary to observe how suddenly the course of the nation was changed from the ascending to the descending plane, along which, but for the valor of our patriot soldiery, it would have been hastened to irretrievable ruin.

Besides the conspicuous contribution to the peace and quiet of the country which Fillmore made by his approval of the compromise measures of 1850, and the

faithful observance of them by his administration, an opportunity was afforded him of showing his high appreciation of the national honor in conducting the relations between the United States and other countries with which
friendly relations existed. While this is a subject which
does not command as much attention from the people as
it should, it nevertheless should not be forgotten that as
we deal with other nations so are they likely to deal with
us. When any nation, in its intercourse with others, intentionally violates the principles of international law it
invites a like violation by such nations as may find it to
their interest to plot against its peace, and, in such cases,
has no just cause of complaint that its own example has
been followed. The occasion here referred to grew out
of the incipient movements designed for the purpose of
annexing the island of Cuba to the United States, a
scheme secretly and adroitly planned during the Polk administration and under his immediate auspices for the sole
purpose of increasing the slave power and so changing
the current of national affairs that it should run in an exclusively southern channel. This is so plain as scarcely
to need explanation. There were then thirty States,
fifteen free and fifteen slave, including Delaware, where
slavery, although nominal, still existed. As Texas was
susceptible of division into at least four States, and Cuba,
if annexed, into at least two more, it was designed, by
the acquisition of that island, to add not less than six
more slave States to the Union, so that there would then
have been twenty-one slave and fifteen free States, the
former having forty-two and the latter thirty Senators.
From a sectional standpoint the stake was worth hard

striving on the part of the South, for, in the event of success, that section of the Union would have had complete control of the government, with the power to dictate its policy, regulate all its affairs and prescribe the conditions upon which new States should be thereafter admitted into the Union.   It does not now require very strong imagination to picture the consequences which would have followed its success.   The whole structure of the government would have been changed.

In 1848, without consulting Congress or giving any notice whatever to the country, Polk instructed the American minister in Spain to offer to purchase Cuba for $100,000,000, although the revenues of the government were steadily diminishing.   When this proposition was made to the Spanish government it was rejected promptly and with indignation.   About that time, and probably with knowledge of this offer, General Narciso Lopez, called a Cuban patriot, inaugurated a revolutionary effort to throw off the Spanish yoke and establish the independence of Cuba.   Failing in this he came to the United States manifestly with the expectation of obtaining assistance in both men and money.   He brought with him other Cubans, whom he employed to represent that the Creole population of Cuba was ready to revolt against the authority of Spain, and, in the event of being successful, desired to be annexed to the United States.   Whatever else may be said of him, he was, doubtless, shrewd enough to understand American politics sufficiently to know that he could enlist the sympathies of the South in his adventure, especially by means of the pretext of annexing Cuba to the United States.

In this he was not mistaken, and if he had reached here during Polk's administration it is as certain as anything not positively demonstrable by proof, that he would not have encountered Presidential hostility, or, at all events, that his appeal for Southern aid could have been enforced by reasons and arguments entirely acceptable to Polk and all the Southern supporters of his administrative policy. However this may have been, he did not reach the United States until shortly before Taylor's death, and made no public demonstration of his purpose until Fillmore became President. He then found existing a very different state of affairs from what he had probably anticipated.

Besides our neutrality laws, the government was forbidden by international comity from interfering with the domestic affairs of Spain, with which country we were at peace. Fillmore placed the highest estimate upon the obligation of obedience to this international comity, and understood it to mean that our intercourse with all nations—of course, including Spain—should be fairly and honorably conducted. Being unwilling that his administration should depart from this obviously proper rule, he issued his official proclamation, April 25, 1851, whereby he forbade that a military expedition should be fitted out in the United States "with intention to invade the island of Cuba, a colony of Spain, with which this country is at peace." Quoting the law which makes such an offense "a high misdemeanor" and subjects those guilty of it to fine and imprisonment, he commanded "every officer of this government, civil or military, to use all efforts in his power to arrest, for trial and punishment, every such offender against the laws of the country.'' The effect of this, however, was limited. In portions of the South circumstances combined to inflame the most restless part of the population, so that a short time after the proclamation the steamer Pampero sailed from New Orleans to Cuba fully equipped with men and arms to aid the Cuban insurrectionists. Whether this could have been prevented or not by greater diligence upon the part of the public officers is now a mere matter of conjecture. But it is unquestionably true that, as the object of Polk in procuring Cuba was to strengthen the slave power, it enlisted the sympathy of so large a portion of the people of the South that they became indifferent to the execution of the neutrality law, and many of them advocated its violation. In one breath they anathematized those of the North who resisted the execution of the fugitive slave law; and in the next vindicated the violation of the neutrality law upon the pretended ground of self-defense—thus justifying the means by the end. The question, therefore, was an embarrassing one, but Fillmore met it in a proper and becoming manner. He communicated the facts to Congress with the recommendation that if, after investigation, the existing law should be found insufficient to suppress such offenses in the future, it should be so amended as to be made effective. It so happened that the expedition from New Orleans proved abortive, for the party was captured by the Spanish authorities in Cuba, and Lopez was executed, by the garrote, in the streets of Havana. But this did not in the least abate the ardor of those in the United States who understood the purposes of Polk's administration. On the contrary, their zeal was increased to such intensity that they succeeded in making the purchase and annexation of Cuba a leading and almost a controlling question in the future politics of the country.

Fillmore was a safe counselor himself, and deeply imbued with the sentiment of national patriotism, and associated with him in his cabinet those whose integrity and ability were vouched for by long public service. These were Daniel Webster, of Massachusetts, Secretary of State, and after his death, October 24, 1852, Edward Everett, of the same State; Thomas Corwin, of Ohio, Secretary of the Treasury; Charles M. Conrad, of Louisiana, Secretary of War; William A. Graham, of North Carolina, Secretary of the Navy; Alexander H. H. Stuart, of Virginia, Secretary of the Interior; Nathan K. Hall, of New York, Postmaster-General, and John J. Crittenden, of Kentucky, Attorney-General. Under their joint guidance, the administration became eminently practical—carefully guarding the national interests alike in every portion of the Union. Sectional agitation having in a great measure abated, although it had not entirely died out—under the beneficent influence of the compromise measures his administration was enabled to employ its official functions for the promotion of the "general welfare." This was accomplished most satisfactorily, and great credit is reflected upon it by the fact that its management of domestic affairs was commended by the country, because when it closed, March 4, 1853, the records of the government did not contain a line or a word upon which the most censorious could rest the accusation of a fault. Nevertheless, his approval

and support of the compromise measures made him adversaries in the North—whose zeal outran their wisdom—
who made the mistake of supposing that the military re-
nown of General Winfield Scott would weigh more in a
Presidential contest than his distinguished civic virtues.
Consequently, in the national convention of 1852, Scott
was nominated over him upon the fifty-third ballot, by
the meager majority of 12, while he never received less
than 112 votes, cast by those who claimed to be, and, in
fact, were, too courageous to play into the hands of any
faction or to surrender principle for expediency.   The
result proved their sagacity, for at the Presidential election of 1852 Scott received the votes of but four out of
thirty-one States—leaving the sectional fanatics of the
South to infer that the sectional fanatics of the North had
no more regard for the Constitution than they had, when
it stood in their way.   Fillmore was in no sense responsible for this—having discharged his duty well and faithfully, he left the responsibility to rest upon others, where
it belonged.   And some of these latter lived long enough
to realize the effects of their error, and to labor industriously and manfully to hold in check the winds which
were uncaged by the election of 1852.

Fillmore was not forgetful of the necessity of extending our commerce to the most remote parts of the world,
and with that view sent a naval expedition to Japan in order, if possible, to bring about commercial intercourse
between that country and the United States.   In this his
success was complete, having been assured by a treaty of
amity, the beneficial effects of which are now visible in

both countries, especially in Japan, where direct commerce with the United States is encouraged and all the rights of American citizens protected. Some years ago, in conversation with the Japanese Minister to this country, a highly cultivated and estimable gentleman, I expressed my surprise that so old a country as Japan had not developed more rapidly, and he replied without hesitation: "You are mistaken in the age of our country, as we only trace its improving condition back a few years—to the time when we entered upon the experiment of imitating the example of the United States." Besides this, he also negotiated commercial treaties with Brazil, Peru and several of the Central American States, from which this country has derived material benefits. And in no respect whatever were any of the important interests pertaining to our trade and commercial intercourse with other nations neglected. Everything within the province and powers of the government was done to accomplish all national objects, and impartial history attests the fact that at no time have our institutions been held in higher estimation throughout the world than they were at the close of his administration. In point of fact the evidences of our internal prosperity were so abundant that they could neither be overlooked nor denied.

The life-work of very few has furnished a fairer and better model for imitation for our young men than that of Fillmore. They can not all become Presidents or members of Congress or eminent lawyers, as he did, but may learn from his example that there is no titled nobility in this country, no law of inheritance which transmits conspicuous stations from parent to child, but that the honor which ennobles its possessor can be won only by the faithful discharge of duty in the various spheres of life, from the highest to the lowest. The poverty of his parents prevented them from giving him even an ordinary education, and at an early age he was apprenticed to learn the fuller's trade. He had a strong natural desire for learning, and the few books he could procure excited this into a passion. In the course of a few years this passion became so absorbing that he induced his employer to release him from the last year of his apprenticeship, and soon fitted himself by untiring perseverance to become the teacher of a common school. As his mind developed and his intellectual vision became broader he chose for his occupation the profession of the law and diligently entered upon its study. After passing the required examination he was admitted to the bar, and in a far shorter time than is common reached an eminent position among the foremost lawyers of New York. After several years of successful practice he was elected to the Congressional House of Representatives, but soon tired of this service, preferring the quiet of home to its turmoil and bustle. His constituents, however, were not willing that he should retire, having learned to appreciate not only his sterling integrity as a man, but his faithful devotion to the public interests as a legislator. They, knowing him as they did, were among the foremost in urging his nomination for the Vice-Presidency, and when he reached the Presidency zealously rallied to the support of his administration, well assured that whatever he did was prompted by the strictest integrity of motive and from the desire to maintain the national honor and perpetuate the Union. Such an attestation of merit is worth far more than partisan applause, and will materially aid in making up the true record of his life. And when that record is impartially made it will prove that, while the intellectual powers of some of our Presidents may have surpassed his, none of them have been more steadfastly devoted to the honor of the nation, the interests of the people and the stability of the Union.

Frank Pierce

CHAPTER XIV

FRANKLIN PIERCE

AT the meeting of the National Convention that nominated Pierce for the Presidency nobody anticipated such a result. It was, therefore, produced entirely by the manipulation of politicians, who regarded the people as standing in the relation to them of " hewers of wood and drawers of water " at their command. How such a thing can occur under institutions supposed to be under popular control is not a little puzzling to the uninitiated, but even these may, after the end has been reached, trace out the inciting motive. If, in this particular instance, the fact shall be demonstrated that the projectors of this movement cherished the secret purpose to violate the compromise measures of 1850 and open again the slavery question, in the face of all its threatening and dangerous consequences, it will go far to fix—if it does not positively fix—upon the proper parties, the revival of the spirit of sectionalism. It is never too late to learn the " truths of history;"—for, whenever known, they lead us into paths which conduct to national security. Even if the past is dead, the present is alive, and the future still before us.

The National Convention that nominated Pierce met at Baltimore, June 1, 1852. The first thing it did was

(333)

to adopt the two-thirds rule which had so effectually disposed of Van Buren in 1844—having been originated
then as a rod to be " held in pickle " over the heads of
such aspirants as exhibited signs of personal independence, or were disposed to be the least refractory.   There
were three avowed candidates—Cass, Buchanan and
Douglas, all men of acknowledged ability and all committed to the support of the compromise measures of 1850, and
thoroughly indoctrinated with the anti-nullification theories which had constituted one of the most distinguishing
characteristics of Jackson's administration.   But neither
of these was satisfactory to the minority—whose votes
were intentionally scattered among half-a-dozen others who
were not candidates, merely, of course, to gain sufficient
time to " stack the cards," at which, from long training,
they had become experts.   The highest vote received at
any time by Cass was 123,—the highest by Buchanan was
104,—and by Douglas was 92.   This continued for 35
ballotings, when, to the surprise of all to whom the secret
had not been confided, Pierce was, for the first time,
brought forward.   This was not done by the delegates
from New Hampshire, where he had lived all his life and
his qualities were well known, but by those from Virginia,
who had accepted the anti-State rights and anti-nullification doctrines of Jackson more from compulsion than
choice, and were vigilant in contriving the means of getting rid of them.   The convention was startled by this
proposition—as the whole country was;—so much so
that it required 14 additional ballots to produce the desired result; and consequently Pierce was not nominated

until the 49th ballot, when he received all the votes cast
except 6, which were still scattering.

There have not been many things in American politics
more inexplicable than this—that is, the selection as a
Presidential candidate of one for whom no demonstration
had been made by the people anywhere, not even in his
own State, over three others much more distinguished,
and whose claims to the nomination had been proclaimed
by large and enthusiastic popular assemblages. What
brought it about was perplexing in the extreme—in fact,
insolvable—even to the politicians who were not admitted behind the screens. But many things have since occurred which make plain and palpable what was then
mysterious.

Pierce was clever—in the sense in which that word im-
ports good-fellowship. His nature was kindly, and he
was so generous-hearted that many of his political adversaries were embraced within the circle of his private
associations—a fact of which I speak from personal experience. His generosity of heart made him impressible
to an unusual degree—especially by those who were
recognized by him as co-operating with him in political
affairs. This was well known to those who procured his
nomination. They knew also that Cass, and Buchanan,
and Douglas, were not the pupils, but leaders, of others—and manifestly ventured upon the selection of Pierce
in preference to either of them, with the hope, if not the
assurance, that, as a new man, brought out from his retirement, he would be more apt to yield to their impor-
tunities than either of these "old stagers," who had well-
matured ideas and projects of their own, and were not

likely to be entrapped into any schemes that would involve conflict with Jackson's anti-nullification opinions
and policy. They were experienced and skillful managers—well-versed in all the arts calculated to assure success—and upon this occasion managed to fill their hands
with trump cards, which they played with wonderful dex-
terity and skill. Pierce had taken no active part in general politics since his retirement from the Senate, ten years
before, and, consequently, had to be, in a large measure,
"taken upon trust," with regard to some of the matters
intended to be then introduced, for the first time, into
the platform upon which the canvass was to be made.
With reference to this, it was supposed that the Presidential office was a stake too highly to be prized for any
analysis of it beyond its general import—or, in apter
words, its "glittering generalities." Consequently, after
condemning "all attempts at renewing in Congress, or
out of it, the agitation of the slavery question, under
whatsoever shape or color the attempt may be made,"
care was taken to add a special pledge to "faithfully
abide by and uphold the principles laid down in the Virginia and Kentucky resolutions" relating to the alien and
sedition laws enacted under the administration of John
Adams, which were declared to be cardinal and fundamental. In this, great ingenuity was displayed by the
concealment, except from the initiated, of a secret purpose it was not considered expedient to avow openly.

The Virginia resolutions referred to—as explained by
Madison—recognized the right of a State to remonstrate
against any law of the United States which impaired its
sovereignty or invaded its legitimate jurisdiction, by in-

voking the aid of the other States, and the employment of all constitutional means to get rid of the obnoxious law. There were two sets of Kentucky resolutions. The first asserted that the Constitution was a compact to which "each State acceded as a State, and as an integral party," and, consequently, had the "right to judge for itself," without regard to what any or all of the other States might do, of any violations of the Constitution of which it should complain, as well as "the mode and measure of redress." Principles in opposition to these were promulgated by legislative resolutions in Delaware, Rhode Island, Massachusetts, New York, Connecticut, New Hampshire, and Vermont; and thereafter there was passed a second set of Kentucky resolutions, which went far beyond those of Virginia, by defining the meaning of the first set, that is, that *"nullification"* of such laws as violate the Constitution "is the rightful remedy." Those who so manipulated this convention as to defeat Cass, Buchanan, and Douglas, and secure the nomination of Pierce, besides being well instructed in all this, knew that the platform would not then be subjected to such critical scrutiny as would expose their ultimate objects. Hence, after the nomination was secured, they indulged in unbounded exultation, because, by courageous persistence through thirty-five ballotings they had secured a Presidential candidate upon a platform in direct conflict with the principles announced by Jackson in his proclamation and message condemning nullification, for which they had cherished against him the most intense hatred, and had been quietly awaiting the time when they could make his allies and sympathizers feel the full force of their ven-

22

geance. It was a severe blow to Cass, Buchanan and Douglas, but especially the latter, who, young, vigorous and talented, had cherished the belief that if the official mantle of the "old hero" should fall upon him there would be no spot or blemish left upon it by any departure from the paths the. latter had marked out for maintaining the life of the nation and holding the States in their constitutional and rightful spheres.

The nomination of Pierce was followed by that of William R. King, of Alabama, for Vice-President, a man of ability and unquestioned integrity, and the canvass resulted in their election by a decided majority. The States then numbered thirty-one, and the whole popular vote was 3,144,201, of which Pierce and King received a plurality of 314,896 over Scott, and a majority of 58,747 over both his competitors, Hale, the abolition candidate, having received 156,149 votes. The only States which gave majorities for Scott were Massachusetts, Vermont, Kentucky and Tennessee—two free and two slave—and it is fair to say that in Kentucky the result was attributable to the influence of Clay, and in Tennessee that respect for the principles inculcated by Jackson and veneration for his memory had not died out. The electoral vote was 254 for Pierce and 42 for Scott, showing that to have been the most remarkable Presidential contest that ever occurred in this country. And that it was in fact so is otherwise proved by its having put again "in the saddle" the politicians whom Jackson had "unhorsed"— that is, the nullifiers, who could then exultingly trace their revival to the secret bargain which, according to Benton, they made with Polk, and which aroused the wrath of

Jackson and led to other consequences heretofore detailed.

At the beginning of his administration, March 4, 1853, Pierce, in his inaugural address, emphatically declared his purpose to maintain the compromise measures of 1850, and to that extent vindicated the wisdom of Taylor and Fillmore, especially of the latter in his official approval of them. That he was sincere in this there is no reason to doubt, for everything he had done and said indicated the desire to maintain the Union by harmonizing the sections. Notwithstanding his own sincerity, however, he was embarrassed in this—that those to whom he was indebted for his nomination, and, in a large measure, for his election, did not take the same view of these compromise measures that he did. They considered them as applicable alone to the free States, as imposing an obligation upon them but no corresponding obligation upon the slave States. Assuming as the postulate of all their arguments that the Constitution gave to the slaveholding States the right to transport their slaves to the Territories and hold them in bondage there, they considered themselves as justified in doing whatever they deemed necessary to maintain this right, even to the extent of enlarging the area of slave territory and strengthening the slave power, while, at the same time, they denied the right of the free States to place any obstacles whatever in the way of accomplishing either or both of these results. If Pierce did not directly affirm this doctrine he acquiesced in it to such an extent that when he afterwards referred to the slavery agitation, after its renewal, he censured the free and exonerated the slave

States on account of it, manifestly desiring to be understood as taking the side of the South against the North.
The faculties of his mind were well developed, but, like
the lawyer who sees only the interest of his client, they
were so warped by his political associations that he was
persuaded to concede to his allies, who had put him in
power, rights and privileges he as readily denied to those
whom he considered as adversaries.   I have stated that,
in my opinion, he was kind-hearted and impressible to
such a degree that he could not resist the earnest en-
treaties of those he considered friends.   This was abundantly proved at the point of his administration I am now
considering, when he seemed to have forgotten that he
was the President of the whole Union and regarded himself as representing alone the interests of the slave section.   This is said without the least disrespect—the feel-
ings I entertain toward him are the reverse of that—for
in no other way is it possible to account for the fact that,
in the face of the compromise of 1850, he secretly employed the authority of his administration to bring about
the annexation of Cuba to the United States, knowing,
as he did, that the only object of it was to strengthen
the slave power, while, at the same time, he heaped his
executive anathemas upon those who resisted this measure upon the ground that such resistance was a violation
of the compromise.   It is impossible not to see now, after the disturbances of that day have been quieted, that
he was induced to regard the compromise as binding
upon the North and not upon the South.   What I have
said about his impressibility is, at least, suggestive, as it
becomes an important factor in the analysis of all indi-

vidual character. There are none who do not feel it in some degree. In our intercourse with the world we all meet with those who attract and those who repel, and toward the former we are drawn by an invisible cord— whether it be called mesmeric or by some other name— through which they convey their sentiments and opinions from their minds to ours, where they remain long enough to become indelible and so to mingle with our own as to become unconsciously an essential part of them. No individual man can break away from this strange and dictatorial influence of friendship, and especially could not Pierce do so, for his sympathetic nature disabled him from detecting the ingeniously contrived processes by which his executive limbs were bound with silken network.

The cabinet of Pierce was composed as follows: William L. Marcy, of New York, Secretary of State; James Guthrie, of Kentucky, Secretary of the Treasury; Jefferson Davis, of Mississippi, Secretary of War; James C. Dobbin, of North Carolina, Secretary of the Navy; Robert McClelland, of Michigan, Secretary of the Interior; James Campbell, of Pennsylvania, Postmaster-General; and Caleb Cushing, of Massachusetts, Attorney-General. Of these Marcy was undoubtedly the ablest man, as he was also fearless and self-willed,—perfectly unbending in the pursuit of his purposes. That he was bold, as well as indifferent to public opinion, was well manifested when— pending the question of confirming the nomination of Van Buren as Minister to England, in January, 1832—he was the first to announce and vindicate the "spoils system" in dispensing official patronage; which he then did, in

the Senate of the United States, by justifying such politicians as "boldly preach what they practice." Then, continuing still further, he said of them: "When they are
contending for victory, they avow their intention of enjoying the fruits of it. If they are defeated, they expect to
retire from office. If they are successful they claim, as a
matter of right, the advantages of success. They see
nothing wrong in the rule that to the victor belong the
spoils of the enemy." A Secretary of State maintaining
these views would be almost certain to impress them upon
the mind of a President like Pierce, and so to shape the
policy of the administration regarding foreign affairs as
to make it conform to his own will. He had James
Buchanan of Pennsylvania as Minister to England; John
Y. Mason of Virginia, Minister to France; and Pierre
Soulé of Louisiana, Minister to Spain. On August 16,
1854, having been, as he declared, "directed by the
President," he addressed an official communication to
the latter, wherein he instructed him to avail himself of
the assistance of both Buchanan and Mason in order to
conduct successfully the negotiations for the purchase of
Cuba from Spain,—with which he had been already
charged, without the direction of Congress or the knowledge of the people. He also directed like instructions to
Buchanan and Mason; and the three were required to
meet at some suitable place in Europe and jointly employ
such means as would bring about the desired result, and
to communicate their proceedings to the Department of
State by a "confidential messenger"—manifestly intending that strict secrecy should be maintained. These
three Ministers held their first meeting at Ostend, in Bel-

gium, which they continued at Aix la Chapelle, in Prus-
sia, and on October 18, 1857, addressed to Marcy, as
Secretary of State, a joint official letter which has become
known as the "Ostend Manifesto." This document is,
to say the least of it, unique in American diplomatic history, and it is creditable to the country that it is so. If
the government of the United States should, by any future possibility, be guided by the course of procedure it
recommends, in its intercourse with other nations, from
that time it would have to rely exclusively upon force
in maintaining its international relations, and would become subject, at all times, to combinations for its overthrow among the strongest and most powerful nations in
the world. For there is nothing plainer or more palpable than that these recommendations do not stop short of
advising that if Spain refuses to sell Cuba, the United
States shall take it by force of arms, in bold and absolute disregard of all national and international rights,—
precisely in accordance with the practice of the highway-
man who stops the traveler upon the road and commands
him "to stand and deliver."

This "manifesto" does not stop at an argument—or
what is designed as such—to prove that it would be to
the interest of Spain and of the United States for the
former to sell and the latter to buy Cuba; but with mar-
velous fatuity, it alleges that our "Union can never en-
joy repose nor possess reliable security so long as Cuba
is not embraced within its boundaries—a proposition the
fallacy of which every average schoolboy in the land can
detect at a glance. Proceeding, then, to show in what
its authors supposed the mutual benefits of the two

countries would consist, it suggests what course the American government should pursue in the event that Spain "should refuse to sell Cuba to the United States." Then, it says, we would be compelled to consider this question: "Does Cuba, in the possession of Spain, seriously endanger our internal peace and the existence of our cherished Union?" And, without the least attempt to show how either of these contingencies could possibly occur, it immediately proceeds to make this startling declaration: "Should this question be answered in the affirmative, then, by every law, human and divine, we shall be justified in *wresting it from Spain, if we possess the power*, and this upon the very same principle that would justify an individual in tearing down the burning house of his neighbor, if there were no other means of preventing the flames from destroying his own house." It requires but little intelligence to see that if we should follow this advice and violate the principles which regulate the international intercourse of modern peoples and our own neutrality laws, we would forfeit our right to complain of the combination of the strong powers against us.

Our government was intended by its founders to be popular in form and substance, and, in order to preserve it as such, the body of the people were made the sovereign source of all its powers, in order that they should be enabled to preserve and perpetuate their own liberties and rights. Originally it was considered an experiment, but at the time of Pierce's administration it was regarded as being no longer so, the preceding sixty-four years of former administrations having demonstrated the capacity

of the people for self-government. Yet, without notice to the country or any attempt to ascertain the
popular will, and without the consent of Congress or
any effort to procure it, these steps for the purchase
of Cuba were all taken in secret, with the hope of
tempting Spain into a treaty by the offer of not less
than $120,000,000 of the public money, having the
Senate ratify the treaty in secret, and then demanding
the payment of the money out of the treasury, upon the
ground that a treaty thus secretly made and ratified, becomes "the supreme law of the land," and binding
upon the country, no matter whether the people or their
immediate representatives in Congress had or had not
any previous knowledge of it, or favored or opposed it.
There would have been no just cause of complaint if the
contemplated treaty had been confined to such matters
as pertain to our ordinary international relations, such as
the protection of our citizens, the enlargement of our
commerce, and other matters legitimately pertaining to
our foreign intercourse, for the Constitution wisely places
these and other kindred affairs within the jurisdiction of
the treaty-making power. But the purchase of Cuba involved the extension of our territorial boundaries, by
stretching them into the ocean so as to embrace territory
not contiguous to the United States, as was the case
when Louisiana, Florida, and a portion of Mexico, were
acquired by treaties. Even in these latter cases the
Constitution was clearly violated, as Jefferson conceded
when Louisiana was procured. The attempt of the
Pierce administration, therefore, to purchase Cuba had

about it none of the merit which attached to the purchase of Louisiana and Florida, because it was, as every
body now knows, a secret effort to violate the compromise of 1850 by adding additional slave territory to the
Union, so that the slave-power should be thereby increased. Pierce's opinions with regard to both the Constitution and the compromise were dictated, not merely
by those he had previously expressed upon the general
question of slavery, but by his immediate relations to
those to whom he felt himself indebted for the Presidential office. Therefore, he seems to have felt himself justified in sending his annual message to Congress, December 4, 1854,—between three and four months after
Marcy's Cuban instructions to Soule—without notifying
Congress and the country of the measures he had secretly
inaugurated and which were then in progress. He did,
however, submit some general reflections, in that message, regarding " the territorial expansion of the United
States," and the "disquieting concern " of "some Eu-
ropean powers " upon that subject. He assigned it to
" the legitimate exercise of sovereign rights " upon our
part,—manifestly intending that what he said should be
understood as relating to past acquisitions. He made no
explanation of the steps then in progress under his own
administration to acquire Cuba; which leaves it fairly to
be supposed that, as he had fully committed himself and
his administration to the maintenance of the compromise
of 1850, it would have been embarrassing to announce
that, to promote the interest of his slave-holding friends
and increase their power in the Union, he was then engaged in efforts to purchase the slave-holding island of

Cuba. I do not say that he intended to deceive the public—for I do not believe he did,—but he was undoubtedly led by partiality for his friends and prejudices against his adversaries, into such a position as required the concealment of his real purposes, in order that the former might obtain a triumph over the latter. It is possible—perhaps probable—that he did not consider the annexation of slave territory a violation of the compromise; at all events, if there is any doubt upon that subject I am disposed to grant him the benefit of it, But however this may have been, the ultimate effect of the attempt to annex Cuba did, when it became exposed, re-open the slave question and justify the free States in protesting against and resisting it.

These two propositions are perfectly clear to my mind: first, that if the letter of the compromise of 1850, strictly interpreted, did not, its spirit did forbid the political re-agitation of the slavery question, both in its general and particular aspects;—and, second, that the slaveholders were not justified in making the clamors of a few factional abolitionists in the North the pretext for plotting secretly to annex Cuba with the view to increase their power while the bulk of the Northern people—truly conservative—continued to acquiesce in the compromise. There were fanatics in the South as well as in the North, and if they had been restrained by the conservatives of the former as they were by the same class in the latter section, the saddest calamities which have since ensued might have been escaped. If Pierce could have anticipated any of these, his patriotism would have incited him to firm resistance to anything tending to that end; but his generosity was so played upon by trained and artful schemers that he suffered his administration to drift along, without intending it, into such lines of policy as opened again the flood-gates of sectional discord, and ultimately caused the waters, which had been dammed up by the compromise, to break loose again and carry desolation to some of the happiest homes in the land.

The troubles which grew out of the organization of Territorial governments for Nebraska and Kansas had their beginning under Pierce's administration, and he very tenaciously adhered to the positions taken by the defenders of slavery. None of the latter were more extreme than he was. All of Nebraska lay above the parallel of 36° 30' north latitude, and the general belief was that the Missouri Compromise, which excluded slavery north of that line of latitude, would have the same effect in that Territory. Hence there had been no controversy relating to the introduction of slavery there. But one was inaugurated pending the Nebraska bill by introducing into it a section which declared the Missouri Compromise "inoperative and void,"—in other words repealing the law of 1820 which established it. This was done first in the Senate, February 15, 1854, by a vote of *yeas* 35, *nays* 10; and in the House of Representatives, May 23, 1854, by a vote of *yeas* 113, *nays* 100. An analysis of these votes will show that, in the Senate, those who voted for this repeal were composed of 22 from the slave and 13 from the free States; and in the House, 68 from the slave and 45 from the free States. And a further analysis will also show that but one Senator from the slave States—Houston of Texas—and but nine Representatives from those States voted against the repeal. From these facts it conclusively appears that the repeal of the Missouri Compromise was brought about by those who represented the slave interest and against the will of those who represented the free North. And when it is considered that this was done in express opposition to the compromise measures of 1850, it does not become those who accomplished it to accuse those who resisted the appeal of sectionalism. The Missouri Compromise had remained undisturbed upon the statute-book for thirty-two years. When enacted it restored peace and quietness to the country, at a time when, without it, the Union might have been imperiled. When repealed under the circumstances here detailed—after the compromise of 1850 had borne good fruits, and while it was still bearing them—it again opened the box of Pandora and scattered its ills throughout the whole country. The question of its constitutionality had been conceded by men of all parties and in all the sections, up till the period when the public peace was disturbed by factional estimates of the value of the Union. The rules of constitutional interpretation had been settled by the highest judicial tribunals in the country and acquiesced in by the National and State Legislatures, as well as by the people generally; but the time had been reached when those who sought after wisdom and enlightenment from these sources were stigmatized as "old fogies," incapable of comprehending the tendency of modern events. A new definition of conservatism was forged; so that instead of implying the desire to preserve as immutable the principles which had the indorsement and approval of "the fathers," it was made to signify such innovation upon those principles as would lead the country into new paths. Stability in government was denounced as delusion, and the wildest experiments were accepted as evidence of statesmanship. In fine, the precepts of the Revolutionary age were considered as relics of the past too hoary to be followed, and designed only to place undue restraint upon the spirit of innovation.

The mind of Pierce was thoroughly inoculated with this spirit of innovation, and accordingly, in his annual message of December 31, 1855, he attempted to prove by a long and labored argument—and I do not doubt the sincerity of his belief that he did prove—that the government of the United States, instead of being a nation co-equal with other nations, is a mere compact or "league" between sovereign and independent States, each one of which requires conformity to its own will, and holds in its hand the rod of chastisement with which to inflict punishment at its own discretion. He applied to the government the term "general," in preference to national, because it signified such limitations upon its powers as to repudiate the idea of sovereignty and substitute for it that of agency and inferiority. Hence, he considered the Congress of the United States as a mere "congress of sovereignties"—that is, of sovereign States —entirely ignoring in this assumption the prominent and controlling fact that, in the preamble to the Constitution, it is expressly and emphatically asserted that the government of the Union was created by "the people of the United States." He displayed both earnestness and ability in promulgating his theories, but suffered his enthusiasm to lead him into the excess of separating the American people entirely from the "general government," and leaving it subject to the dominion of the "sovereign States"—for, if the people of the States have alone formed their State governments, and these, as such, have entered into a compact or league of "general government," then it is false and misleading to say that there is any such political community as the people of the United States in any other sense than as they are the people of the several States, incapable of aggregation for the purposes of government, or with any other view than mere statistical enumeration.

By this fallacious method of reasoning, which had been exploded by all his predecessors from Washington down, he persuaded himself to the conclusion that the Missouri Compromise was unconstitutional and congratulated the country upon its repeal. This was not unexpected, for by that time he had become accustomed to employ arguments, almost *ex parte*, in favor of the slaveholders, apparently unconscious of the fact that citizens of the free States had any interest whatever in the common property of the nation. The process of reasoning he adopted was equally well calculated to prove that the celebrated ordinance of 1787, for the government of the Northwestern Territory, was also unconstitutional, and that the States which had been formed out of that Territory could constitutionally have been made slave States, in disregard of its provisions. With whatever earnestness and sincerety he may then have done this, it is easy now to see, after the animosities of that period have been extinguished, that the immediate effect was to satisfy slaveholders that their efforts to carry slaves to the Territories and to hold them there as such, under the protection of the "general government," did not violate the compromise of 1850, but that efforts upon the part of citizens of the free States to prevent this, even by fair and legitimate means, were violative of that compromise. What he said was equivalent to saying that the compromise measures of 1850 were binding upon the North but not upon the South. And such was the manifest import of all the reasoning of this well-written message, as well as of that which followed it, as will now appear to any dispassionate reader who will carefully and intelligently scrutinize the contents of both. His zeal in behalf of those who had brought him out of retirement and made him President far exceeded any he displayed for the nation at large, not because he harbored in his mind any hostility to the Union, but because he allowed his attachment for these friends, in obedience to the dictates of his impressible nature, to close his eyes to their excesses and minimize their faults, while, at the same time, he magnified those of their Northern antagonists. Such impulsive acquiescence in the suggestions which spring from private intercourse and friendship is not only commendable, but proves the possession of natural qualities of head and heart which tend to refine and elevate their possessors. They are unsuited, however, to the public affairs of State, because individuals alone are not concerned in these—they influence the interests and fortunes of whole populations. I am willing to believe that Pierce may not then have considered his sectional utterances intemperate or uncalled for, but rather as the outburst of a sympathetic heart.   But scrutinized now, in the light of the events which have since occurred and have become integral parts of our history, his eloquent advocacy of the exorbitant demands of his Southern friends and allies appears more like the personal defense of a cause he believed to be enfeebled by the imprudent zeal of its sectional defenders, than the dispassionate argument of a statesman who felt himself inspirited by the broad and comprehensive sentiments of nationality.

The controversy in Nebraska and Kansas was well calculated to put both the patience and patriotism of Pierce to a severe test.   The indiscreet and unwise repeal of the Missouri Compromise opened both of those Territories to the introduction of slavery, if it was not actually intended to invite it.   Consequently, a direct issue was made between freedom and slavery, which involved two controlling considerations,—first, the humanitarian aspects of slavery as a permanent institution, and, second, the enlargement and increase of the slave power, so as to give it complete and perpetual dominion over national affairs. Without any present regard to the former of these considerations, it is sufficient to say of the latter that it forced upon the country a question of vast importance to every section, and this in palpable violation of the compromise of 1850, as well as the dictates of patriotism and prudence.   The natural and inevitable effect was to incite the desire upon the part of Northern and Southern populations to occupy the Territories—the former to keep them free and the latter to convert them into slave States.   Among these populations the Northern were more accustomed to emigration to the Northwest than

23

the Southern,—mainly to better their temporal condition and fortunes. In the South, however, a new motive for increased and increasing emigration arose out of the political desire to give to that section the controlling influence over national affairs, and this motive was entirely independent of the desire to better the temporal condition of the emigrant. In each section the managers urged their respective adherents forward to fight the great political battle—not caring, in the least, whether they procured permanent homes or not. They sent them as political missionaries—some for the cause of freedom, others for that of slavery—and held themselves in reserve for enjoying, at their own homes, but in neither Nebraska nor Kansas, the fruits of such political victory as was won. It was strange infatuation which caused this fierce struggle to be recognized as territorial only;—it was national both in its immediate bearings and its ultimate consequences. If the South had won, slavery would have become the controlling condition in territorial settlement and organization, while freedom would have been the exception. But the South did not win; and those who remember that controversy, or shall acquire accurate information of it from the history of that period, can not escape the conviction that to the same misguided zeal which brought it on is the South alone indebted for the ultimate extirpation of slavery.

It was not owing to Pierce that the South did not succeed. If any reader capable of verbal analysis will read his special message to Congress, dated January 24, 1856, he will find that he assigns the troubles in Kansas partly to "local mal-administration," but in a greater degree to "the unjustifiable interference of the inhabitants of some of the States foreign by residence, interests, and rights to the Territory." If the reader of this message will pause at this point he will be inclined to agree with and commend him for excluding from Kansas the slavery propagandists from just across the Missouri boundary-line, as well as the free-State missionaries from New England. But if he will read a little further he will see that while he regards both of these classes as "foreign by residence," he considers the New Englanders as unauthorized and unjust intermeddlers, and justifies the Missourians, because they were "near to the Territory of Kansas," and the people of the latter "were to become their neighbors;" as if the rights of citizenship upon questions concerning the welfare of the nation were hedged in by the boundary lines between the States, or between them and the Territories. Inasmuch, therefore, as the "domestic peace" of Missouri would be "most directly endangered" by making Kansas a free State, his zeal in behalf of the extension of slavery so infatuated him—unconsciously, no doubt—that he could not realize his own official inconsistency, which everybody else could see.

But no matter now for this. Pierce was honest in his opinions and in the expression of them. To him they doubtless seemed justified and sustained by the existing condition of the country. Possibly, if he had lived a few years longer, his fine intellect, matured by still greater experience, would have enabled him to realize that some of the things I have pointed out as errors of administration were truly so. At all events, when the War of the Rebellion broke out and his former allies in the South made an effort to pull down the pillars upon which the National Union was resting, he raised his eloquent voice in condemnation of the act, and implored the people of his native State to stand by the national cause and lend a helping-hand to the government in maintaining the Union. If he spoke kind words to his old friends of the South, his sentiments were controlled and dominated by the desire to see the national cause triumphant. If he did not live long enough to witness all the fruits which that triumph has borne, he did not go to his final sleep until it became complete. And now that I have survived him, and have expressed my opinion of his public acts with both freedom and candor, I can not close without saying that, as a personal friend whose private virtues and generous impulses I admired, my hope is that he may be sleeping sweetly.

James Buchanan

CHAPTER XV

JAMES BUCHANAN

MANY now living have no personal knowledge of the terrible internecine struggle into which this country was plunged by the sectional infatuation of Southern politicians, about the close of Buchanan's administration, and many others have but shadowy remembrance of its causes. Some of these were remote, others immediate; but whether the one or the other, their culmination then makes that period not only one of the most important in our recent history, but difficult of detailed and satisfactory explanation. There may be discovered, however, evidences to show that Buchanan was surrounded by many serious and trying embarrassments,—such as none of his predecessors encountered. That he was held responsible for many things not justly chargeable against him is probably true, in view of the intense excitement which prevailed. Yet, at the same time, the actual "truth of history" assigns to him a feebleness of purpose and timidity of conduct, which contributed in a large degree to results that might have been escaped by bold and intrepid action upon his part. It ought not to be said of him that he sympathized with the *objects* of the rebellion,—for the supposition that he was willing to contribute knowingly anything to the overthrow of the

(357)

Union would be, in my opinion, both unjust and unmerited. But it is not easy to escape the conviction that he temporized with those to whom he was indebted for the Presidential office to such a degree that his administration became powerless to encounter their disunion plottings, and contributed, without his intending it, to the end they sought after. Unexpected consequences often follow a combination of causes, as surprising to those who aided in producing the combination as to others. This, it is fair to say, was the condition in which Buchanan was placed more by the contrivances of others than by himself. Much of the wrong he did he believed to be right, and acting under this conviction, he pursued his course to a dangerous extremity, doubtless hoping that at last all sectional wounds would be healed, and his wisdom justified by the removal of every cause of sectional disturbance and the complete vindication of the integrity of the Union. Whatever I may once have thought and said, when the light did not shine as clearly upon his administration as it does now, I am unwilling to withhold this voluntary tribute to his patriotic purposes. "Let justice be done though the heavens fall." Justice is represented as a blind goddess, holding at perfect equipoise the scales with which she weighs the merits and demerits of us all, and now when each fleeting day makes more apparent the faults I have myself committed, I am admonished of the duty and obligation of dealing generously with those of others. At the time of their occurrence many of the acts of Buchanan's administration seemed to me not only hurtful to the country, but unpardonable. But it may have been that my own attachment to the Union was such that I erroneously supposed I saw signs of hostility to it, when he was striving with perfect sincerity, by instrumentalities he deemed would be effective, for its perpetual preservation.

The national convention which nominated Buchanan for President met at Cincinnati June 2, 1856. His chief competitor was Pierce, whose friends urged his selection with great earnestness and zeal, because they considered it important that the policy of his administration should be indorsed, inasmuch as a departure from it would disarrange their plans for the future. Douglas and Cass were also voted for, but the main contest was between Buchanan and Pierce. Many of the ballotings were merely experimental until after the fifteenth, when the friends of Pierce, finding his nomination impossible, withdrew his name and left the contest between Buchanan and Douglas, as Cass was at no time a formidable competitor. On the sixteenth ballot Buchanan received 168 votes, Douglas 121 and Cass 6, which gave the former a majority of 41 of the whole vote and led to his unanimous nomination on the next or seventeenth ballot. Whereupon John C. Breckinridge, of Kentucky, was nominated for Vice-President. A platform was then adopted which, upon general subjects, did not materially differ from that of 1852, upon which Pierce had been elected. It repeated what was there said condemnatory of slavery agitation, strangely ignoring the prominent fact that those who composed the convention and their friends and allies had caused the Missouri Compromise to be repealed, and had themselves thus revived the slavery agitation after it had been quieted by the compromise of 1850. And besides, with equal obtuseness, the platform continued this agitation by taking the side of and encouraging those who were then striving, with or without law, to make Nebraska and Kansas slave States and vigorously censured those who were trying to make them free. In its special features upon these exciting subjects it was flagrantly sectional, rivaling in this respect some of the declarations put forth by those who claimed to be distinctively abolitionists.

Why Buchanan should have been preferred to Pierce, in view of the course of the latter's administration, was not then easy to explain. The problem is more solvable now. He had been personally engaged, while minister to England—along with our ministers to France and Spain—in negotiating for the purchase of Cuba, and was the author of the "Ostend manifesto." Inasmuch, therefore, as this purchase was considered essential to the increase of the slave power by adding slave territory to the Union, it was manifestly believed that his familiarity with the question, as well as with the diplomatic methods of influencing the Spanish authorities, would afford him such facilities when President as would give better promise of success under his than under Pierce's administration, inasmuch as the latter had attempted the negotiation and failed. Besides, there was another consideration regarded as favorable to Buchanan. He had been, in early life, what was known as a Federalist, and had won his first distinction as the advocate of a strong national government and the consequent weakening of the powers of the State governments. He had been accustomed to construe the Constitution so as to justify the exercise of implied powers to such an extent as the "general welfare" required. But he had abandoned this method of constitutional interpretation and adopted the opposing theory, which weakened the National Government and strengthened the State governments. He was not charged with insincerity, nor was his integrity impeached in consequence of this change; yet, like other zealous converts to new opinions, he pursued the State-rights line of thought and argument, after adopting it, until he became recognized as one of the ablest among the Northern defenders of the doctrines embodied in the Kentucky and Virginia resolutions. Hence, as these resolutions had been introduced into the platform of 1852 and were repeated in that of 1856, it was fitting to give him preference over Pierce, who, while he accepted them as containing true doctrines, had not been so conspicuously their advocate as he had. In fact, no other politician of the North had rivaled Buchanan in this respect, and not very many in the South; so that his nomination was an admirable stroke of policy upon the part of those who were then exerting their utmost power and taxing all their energies, to lessen the powers of the National Government by increasing those of the State governments, to such an extent that Nebraska and Kansas should be made slave States and future territorial organizations so regulated as to assure the permanent triumph of the slave over the free States in subsequent sectional contests for political power.

Before the nomination of Buchanan and Breckinridge, a national convention assembled in Philadelphia, February 19, 1856, and nominated Millard Fillmore, of New York, for President, and Andrew J. Donelson, of Tennessee, for Vice-President; and another which afterwards met also at Philadelphia, June 17, 1856, nominated John C. Fremont, of California, and William L. Dayton, of New Jersey, for the same offices. There were thus three presidential candidates, and that fact was considered favorable to Buchanan, inasmuch as those upon whose support he relied were too earnest in the pursuit of a common object to allow their ranks to be divided, whereas his opponents were not united by any binding tie. The public expectation was fulfilled by his election, although it was additional evidence to show how a candidate who receives a minority of the popular vote may be constitutionally elected President. Of the popular vote then cast he received 1,836,169, Fremont 1,341,264, and Fillmore 874,531. Consequently, while Buchanan received a plurality of 496,905 over Fremont, he fell 377,626 short of a majority of votes polled. The slave States voted solidly for Buchanan, except Maryland, which gave a majority of 8,064 for Fillmore. In ten of them Fremont did not receive a single vote, while in Kentucky he received 314, Maryland 281 and Virginia 291—making only a total of 886 out of more than 1,000,000 votes cast in the slave States. When, therefore, we take into consideration the fact that Buchanan was running upon a platform which emphatically indorsed the sentiments of the South and the further fact that he received in the North majorities aggregating over 750,000, this insignificant vote of Fremont was not merely absolute proof of sectionalism in the South, but an invitation to like sectionalism in the North,—if, indeed, it were not the outgrowth of a defiant spirit. There are not many persons so tame as to submit quiescently to either indignities or blows from such as employ them to indicate either antagonism or hostility,—and aggregated communities never do, because a common instinct incites them to resistance. Nevertheless, Buchanan received 174 electoral votes, Fremont 114, and Fillmore 8,—which gave him a majority of 52 over both and entitled him constitutionally and legally to the Presidential office.

His inaugural address, delivered March 4, 1857, was clear and sufficiently concise,—exhibiting great ability, for which due credit was universally given to him. The reference it contained to slavery agitation was appropriate and satisfactory to the public. While he made no allusion to the violation of the compromise of 1850 by the repeal of the Missouri Compromise, whereby the whole question of slavery in its manifold bearings was reopened by those who had elected him, he did display some impatience at the condition of the country, which he afterwards attributed mainly to that repeal. He expressed the belief, however, that the true solution of the difficulty regarding slavery in the Territories was dependent upon the ultimate decision of the people of each Territory. This he called "popular sovereignty,"—entirely distinguished from the "squatter sovereignty" doctrine of Douglas in this, that while the latter recognized the right of the people of a Territory to admit or exclude slavery at any period of their territorial existence, his doctrine confined the exercise of that right to the time when they were authorized by law to form a constitution preparatory to admission into the Union as a State. This was a proper and commendable display of wisdom upon his part, but it is not probable he would have made the issue between these two theories so direct and palpable as he did by his inaugural, if he could have foreseen the consequences to which it ultimately and inevitably led. Nevertheless, it is possible that he then merely intended to rebuke the excesses and intemperance of those whose extreme violence had produced threatening complications in Nebraska and Kansas—more especially in the latter. This is as far as he could go with propriety in an inaugural, which is understood to deal only with generalities,—among which he evidently classed the proposition laid down by him with so much emphasis,—that the people of a Territory when forming a State constitution, but at no other time, have the complete and exclusive power to settle the question of slavery for themselves.

There was one portion of the inaugural especially significant to those who were admitted behind the screens, but which to those who were not was altogether unmeaning, except as boastful exultation at the "glory" we had achieved in extending our territorial limits "by fair purchase," while such other nations as did so had enlarged "their dominions by the sword." The public accepted this as they would a beautifully rounded period in a Fourth of July address, but the politicians who had defeated Pierce and planned the nomination and election of Buchanan understood it to mean, as it undoubtedly did, the purchase of Cuba. They had set their hearts upon that measure, and Buchanan well understood that they would

invoke the employment of all his executive powers to accomplish it, and hence he considered it advisable, at the
beginning of his administration, to avow his readiness to
comply with the condition—whether express or implied
no matter—which had borne so conspicuous a part in de-
feating Pierce and in securing his own nomination and
election.   Consequently, when continuing, he said: ''No
nation will have a right to interfere or to complain if, in
the progress of events, we shall still further extend our
possessions,'' he furnished his pro-slavery allies the
strongest possible inducement for rallying to the support
of his administration, and was thus enabled to start out
with the most flattering prospects of complete success.

It would serve no valuable purpose now to revive, in
the minds of any, recollection of the multitude of events
which grew out of the Kansas embroglio, and, like leaden
weights, dragged down the administration of Buchanan.
They served, for a time, the bad purpose of convulsing
the nation to its utmost extremities, and those of the
present day who should undertake to discover the truth
in the mass of chaotic materials would be likely to find
themselves lost in an inextricable labyrinth.   There are,
however, some prominent facts, not disputed, which
clearly show the extent to which Buchanan employed his
executive power exclusively in behalf of those who endeavored, by fair means or foul, to force slavery upon
the Kansas people.   That he condemned the North and
applauded the South in all that was done by the two
classes of disputants no ingenuous man will deny.   As
he hated the abolitionists of the North with an intense
hatred, he classed with them every man, whether in or

out of Kansas, who advocated a free-State constitution, and held himself in constant readiness to consign them to the hottest fires of persecution. To him the unsworn statement of a single advocate of slavery was worth more than piles of affidavits from the friends of freedom. To him an abolitionist was a leper, to be shunned and avoided as one who propagated a fatal disease. The fact that such a man was a *bona fide* citizen of Kansas and had secured to him by law the undoubted right to vote, was of no consequence, when his vote counteracted the influence of the propagandist of slavery specially imported from Missouri and other slave States. To him the Topeka Constitution was revolutionary and lawless and the Lecompton Constitution was lawful and right, notwithstanding the former was an effort of the free-State population to protect themselves from armed bands carried there to establish slavery, and the latter had its inception and origin in a "reign of terror," not of the same proportions as the Commune of Paris, but akin to it.

These things are of but little importance now, except as they serve to show how the strongest minds are sometimes influenced and warped by political ambition, and as helps to a proper understanding of Buchanan's leading characteristics. He was opposed to slavery upon principle,—as he often declared, when it was proper for him to do so. But in order to supplant Pierce and reach the Presidency—the *ultima thule* of his political ambition— he had permitted himself to become entangled in an alliance with those whose chief object was its extension and perpetuation, and consequently the principle involved became of secondary import when compared with his own personal success. He was tightly bound with cords which could only be unloosed by those who wound them around him, and this they were unwilling to do until their ends were accomplished. Before his captivity, his vigorous mind had enabled him to see clearly that, by the covenant of union when the government was formed, the right to hold their slaves was guaranteed to the slave States; but after that his intellectual vision became so changed that he thought he saw that, within this constitutional right, there was included the additional right to extend slavery wherever beyond these original State boundaries the interest of slave-holders, or the cupidity of slave-dealers, might require. How this could be done consistently with the obligation to maintain freedom in preference to slavery, as a matter of principle, he could then see for the first time,—notwithstanding, in order to see it, the perversion of his highest intellectual faculties was required. There was nothing puzzling in this perversion, when ambition presided over the court where these faculties were invoked, enlarging some, dwarfing others, but taking care to maintain its own ascendancy over all. And thus Buchanan became himself a slave—a slave to his ambition—and was so obedient to those who had the Presidential office to dispense, as to become persuaded that, although slavery was wrong upon principle, it would be right to extend the wrong provided it would assure his election to the Presidency. He could not wait much longer. Age was beginning to show its ravages upon his once robust frame. The luster of his eye was becoming somewhat dimmed. If he waited four years more, when he would

be almost three score and ten, other and younger competitors would be likely to step in before him.   That was
his last chance.   And, consequently, he was ready to accept any terms and conditions the slave-power might
prescribe in order to reward his ambition.   By no other
method of reasoning than this could he account, even to
himself, for having consented to become the executive
commander of the sectional forces combined to extend
slavery—*vi et armis*, if necessary—beyond the limits of
the slave States.

The cabinet of Buchanan shows a tendency to extremes,—not to disunion, for with that sentiment I am
convinced he did not sympathize—but with regard to
such measures as the interests of the slave-holding section dictated, no matter how those of the free-State section might be affected.   His cabinet was as follows:
Lewis Cass of Michigan, Secretary of State; Howell
Cobb of Georgia, Secretary of Treasury; John B. Floyd
of Virginia, Secretary of War; Isaac Toucey of Connecticut, Secretary of the Navy; Jacob Thompson of Mississippi, Secretary of the Interior; Aaron V. Brown of
Tennessee, Postmaster-General, and Jeremiah S. Black
of Pennsylvania, Attorney-General.   My personal acquaintance with all these gentlemen—which was intimate
with three of them—enables me to bear testimony to
their ability and high character.   I say this with pleasure, and the more willingly as I have survived them all.
At the same time, however, it will be observed at a
glance that out of the seven members who composed the
cabinet four of them—a majority—were representatives
of the pro-slavery sentiments and opinions of the South,

and had charge of the finances, military affairs, all matters connected with the public lands and Indian tribes,
and the post-office system—which embraced almost the
entire interior and domestic workings of the government,—while to the remaining three were confided foreign affairs, naval affairs, and the law department, which
were separated almost entirely from these interior and
domestic matters, except in so far as occasional questions of law arose. All of these four cabinet counselors
had persuaded themselves to believe, and were united in
the belief that the North was hostile to the South, and
were, for that reason, hostile to the North. As everybody knew this in those days, it is fair to accept it as a
'' fixed fact.'' Hence the conclusion can not be escaped,
that in the management of their several departments,
they gave preference to the South over the North, in all
matters where the question of slavery was either directly
or indirectly involved. In this they were governed by an
inflexible law which regulates human conduct,—whereby the actions of individuals become responsive to their
purposes and intentions. Therefore, as, with each one
of them, the interests and welfare of his section—possibly of his State—were positively controlling, all matters
pertaining to slavery were considered from a sectional
standpoint, and the ordinary affairs of administration
were so conducted as to assure to the South the advantage over the North. All questions that arose, outside
these ordinary administrative matters, were political in
their nature and all the explanations of them were sectional in character. Those members of the cabinet who
represented the slave-holding interests were undoubtedly
24

united, and perfectly well understood the advantages to
be derived from that union. These men were bold,
while Buchanan was timid,—and were entirely familiar
with all the plans and methods by which boldness almost invariably wins the victory over timidity, in the
conduct of political affairs. Hence, it is not at all surprising that Buchanan—dominated over by these courageous
advisers—permitted his administration to maintain and
vindicate all the extreme measures of the pro-slavery
men in the Territories—especially in Kansas—and sent
out violent anathemas against the free-State men. He
ought to have seen that those who were dictating the
policy of his administration were already beginning to
calculate the value of the Union. I am willing to believe that he did not see this, but, on the other hand,
that he yielded to those who had stronger will power
than he had. There is no keen observer of human nature who has not known men endowed with the highest
faculties of mind become so listless with regard to the
current of passing events as to suffer them to drift to
ends they did not anticipate, and who have been awakened to the actual reality by the crashing of the wrecks
around them. To say this of Buchanan as President is
to put a charitable construction upon his conduct and intentions, which, with every frank and candid mind, is pref-
ferable to harsh criticism and censure.

Buchanan was sensitive with regard to the position his
administration would be likely to occupy in history; but,
perhaps, not unduly so. While he was yet President, the
State of South Carolina and other States which had cast
their electoral vote for him had passed legislative ordi-

nances seceding from the Union—in other words, making an effort to dissolve it. As this disloyal step was taken by those who had contributed to his election, he undoubtedly feared,—if he did not, in fact, apprehend,— that public opinion would hold him, in a large degree, responsible, inasmuch as the events occurred during his administration. Consequently, after his retirement from the Presidency, he prepared at Wheatland, his home, a history, or defense, of his administration, which was published in 1866, in a volume of 296 pages. That he was the author of this work is plainly shown in the preface, where, speaking of himself in the third person, he says that he withheld the publication rather than "embarrass Mr. Lincoln's administration," and because "the author deemed it far better to suffer temporary injustice than to expose himself to such a charge." And, in order to make himself more explicit, while still alluding to the author, he adds: "He therefore claims the merit—if merit it be simply to do one's duty—that whilst in the exercise of executive functions he never violated any of its provisions"—meaning the Constitution. A strong necessity must, in his opinion, have demanded this defense, inasmuch as none of his predecessors had set such an example. He could easily see, however, that his attitude differed from theirs materially, in this,—that none of the friends and supporters of any previous administration had ever gone to the extremity of enacting an ordinance of secession. They who had done so then were the immediate descendants and followers of those who ventured to go to the extent of nullification under Jackson. But, in resorting to this method of defense, he

exhibited a thorough consciousness of the difference between himself and the "old hero,"—that is, that while
the latter seized the hilt of his sword at the first threat of
rebellion against the Union, he had "faltered in a double
sense" with these same aggressors until there was left to
him no other weapon but his pen.   No matter, however,
about the difference between Jackson and Buchanan—in
the measurement of which the most vivid imagination
would be balked—it is sufficient for us now to recognize
this volume, prepared by the latter's own hand, as expressing accurately the views he entertained of his own
administrative policy and the condition of the country
while he was President and until the close of his administration.   If it were read by every intelligent voter in
the United States, and the whole population should be
required to render a verdict based upon its contents, that
verdict would be, that the divisions and angry disputes
among those who elected him President were the primary and inciting causes of South Carolina's secession:
and that his own executive timidity led, as naturally as
effect follows cause, to results he may not have foreseen
and did not desire,—that is, to the secession of other
States and to civil war.

He denounces with severity the abolitionists of the
North, and includes among them all who did not support
his administrative policy, thus not merely excusing but
justifying the clamorous accusations of the pro-slavery
agitators of the slave States and their Northern allies.
He alludes, in commendation and approval, to the proceedings in Kansas which led to the adoption of the Lecompton Constitution, establishing slavery, and disap-

provingly to those which led to the Topeka Constitution, creating a free State, and explains the reasons why he approved the former and opposed the latter. He gives his express sanction to the decision of the Supreme Court of the United States in the celebrated Dred Scott case, to the effect that the slaveholders of the Southern States had the constitutional right to take their slaves to any of the Territories and hold them there as such. He arraigns Douglas and his followers along with the abolitionists for having "disregarded" this decision by their "squatter sovereignty" doctrine to the effect that the people of a Territory, during their territorial existence, have the right to enact organic laws either admitting or rejecting slavery as they see fit—seemingly, in this, unconscious of the palpable fact that if the Constitution secured this right it could no more be taken away by the people of a Territory when they formed their State Constitution than before, for the plain reason that existing constitutional rights are not dependent, in any sense, upon either State or Territorial assent. His arraignment of Douglas and his supporters in the Presidential canvass of 1860 borders closely upon fierceness. Still referring to the Dred Scott decision, he says: "They treated it as though it had never been made, and still continued to agitate without intermission and with powerful effect until the very day of President Lincoln's election," while those who followed him in yielding "a willing obedience to the decision of the Supreme Court" adhered tenaciously to the "ancient and time-honored principles in support of law and order," which had been established by the party he was serving and to which Douglas pro-

fessed to belong. The immediate effect of this diver-
gence of views between him and his friends and Douglas
and his friends—as he manifestly supposed he had
pointed out distinctly—was to exasperate "the Southern
people" and place "in the hands of Southern disunion
agitators a powerful weapon against the Union." And
inasmuch as he did not permit this volume to pass out of
his hands until just after the close of the civil war, he
deemed it necessary to vindicate his opinions and the
policy of his administration by declaring that the war
"would most probably never have existed had not the
American people disobeyed and resisted the Constitution
of their country as expounded by the tribunal which they
themselves had created for this express purpose"—that
is, the Dred Scott decision, which authorized the holding of slaves throughout every foot of the territory of the
United States. This is precisely as if he had said that
Douglas and his supporters in 1860 did their full share,
together with those he called abolitionists, towards bring-
ing on the civil war. And it is also an arraignment of
Jackson, his administration and his multitude of defenders for their like disregard of the decision of the Supreme Court of the United States upon the constitutionality of a national bank. How marvelously strange such
things now appear, when reason, remounting her throne,
has quieted the passions of that period!

With this premise to build upon he proceeds to offer
proof in verification of his convictions. After pointing
out the tendency of the North to abolitionism and at-
tributing this to Seward's "Irrepressible Conflict" and to
Helper's "Impending Crisis,"—as if the conflict had

been inaugurated alone by the North, while the South had always been quiescent and composed,—he carries his readers to the national convention that met in Charleston, South Carolina, April 23, 1860, to nominate his successor to the Presidency. A careful reading of what he has said concerning this body will show that he has considered it from the pro-slavery standpoint exclusively, whereas it is clearly demonstrated by its proceedings that it was the most absolutely sectional assemblage of politicians that had ever met in the United States, in so far as its character is to be decided by its acts. No intelligent man can examine its proceedings, as they were officially announced, without seeing that it constituted an important turning-point in American politics, as well as a danger-signal, which, like one erected to warn the mariner of the coming storm, notified the country that the enemies of the Union were sharpening their swords to cut its silken cords. It was known to be composed of warring elements,—for undoubtedly there were many there who did not sympathize with this unpatriotic design,—and the reconciliation of this discord was professedly its main object. In this self-exculpatory volume of Buchanan he endeavors to explain the origin and causes of this discord, plainly with the purpose of removing from himself and his administration any censure whatever on account of it, so that it may rest, with all the odium attaching to it, upon Douglas and his friends,—for that he puts them in the same class with the abolitionists, as mischievous agitators of the slavery question, is a plain and indisputable fact. He says of those who were endeavoring to persuade this convention to nominate Douglas for

the Presidency, as his successor, that they were "strong-
ly tinctured with an anti-slavery spirit,"—meaning thereby that they did not sufficiently repel the abolitionists,
because they were somewhat in sympathy with them.
And he gives this as the ground of his accusation: that
they "maintained the power of a territorial legislature to
impair or destroy slave property," which was equivalent
to saying that all the Territories were, by the Constitution, open to the introduction of slavery at the discretion
of the Southern slaveholders, who therefore possessed
the incontestable power and right to make slave States of
them.   In this he dealt with Douglas and his supporters
precisely as the pro-slavery men of the South did, he and
they taking special care to omit the important facts that
the "squatter sovereignty" theory of Douglas recognized
also the right of the people of the Territories to author-
ize and establish slavery, and that upon this point Douglas and the abolitionists were separated as widely as the
poles.   I do not think it necessary to inquire into the
justice or injustice of this, inasmuch as the mere statement of the facts conclusively show, first, the fierce war
upon Douglas in the Charleston convention by Buchanan
and his administration; and, second, the origin of the
division and separation of their respective friends, which
added fuel to the flames of sectional strife and brought
on the civil war, which but for this would never have
occurred, or might have been avoided.   I have said of
Buchanan that, in my belief, he would knowingly have
done nothing to positively endanger the Union.   But the
foregoing events, and others to which they were intimate-
ly related, teach this lesson, that he unconsciously yielded

to the imperious and persistent demands of those sectional leaders who played with his weak and vacillating purposes as the harper plays upon the strings of his harp. It was otherwise with Douglas. With him love of the Union was an intense passion, which had "grown with his growth and strengthened with his strength." His convictions were sincere and his courage so unshaken that it protected him against all the machinations of those who were plotting against the Union. Of this the history of this Charleston convention furnishes satisfactory proof; for it is well understood that if he had then assented to the extreme opinions of the South, as Buchanan did, his nomination for the Presidency would have been assured, and that his refusal to do so caused his defeat.

One of the important steps taken by this convention was to provide that a vote of two-thirds of the delegates should be required to make a nomination. As all the States were represented and there were 303 delegates, it therefore required that 202 votes should be necessary to a choice. Although this rule had been acquiesced in since 1844, when it was introduced to defeat Van Buren and nominate Polk in order to assure the annexation of Texas and the increase of the slave power to that extent, it was then considered by the pro-slavery delegates as absolutely essential to the defeat of Douglas, and, cautiously concealing this purpose, they succeeded in having it specially provided for. It was decided that a nomination should not be made until a platform had been agreed upon, and a committee composed of one delegate from each State was appointed to construct one. On the fifth day of the convention this committee made majority and minority reports, the former approving the decision of the Supreme Court in the Dred Scott case and the latter the "squatter sovereignty" doctrine of Douglas. This made the issue distinct and emphatic, as it was represented on one side by Buchanan and his administration and on the other by Douglas and his friends. After an exciting discussion a vote was taken upon these reports, the result of which was that 165 approved the minority report and 138 that of the majority, a majority of 27 in favor of the doctrine maintained by Douglas and against that maintained by Buchanan. Upon this vote the delegates from the following slave States—Maryland, Virginia, Missouri, Tennessee and Kentucky—were divided, but with these exceptions the slave States were united in favor of the majority report. These facts demonstrate that if instead of requiring two-thirds a majority had been permitted to control, consistently with one of the fundamental principles of popular government, Douglas would have received the nomination. And if this had occurred and the South had acquiesced in it, as fidelity to the Union demanded, the peace of the country would have remained unbroken, for whether Douglas had been elected or defeated, slavery in the States would have been protected by an observance of all the constitutional guarantees. But those delegates who maintained the theory of Buchanan were resolved that he should not be nominated, and that as they then had a President who maintained their right to carry their slaves to all or any of the Territories and hold them there, they did not intend that any man should be nominated who would not consent to run upon a platform to that effect. As the adoption of the minority report had convinced them that this could not be accomplished, they resorted to the extreme measure of breaking up the convention. Accordingly, on April 30, after the body had been in session one week, the delegates from Louisiana, Alabama, South Carolina, Mississippi, Florida, Texas and Arkansas withdrew. After these and a few other withdrawals special action upon the two-thirds rule was had in order to assure conclusively the defeat of Douglas. Referring to it Buchanan himself says its adoption ''rendered the regular nomination of Mr. Douglas impossible,'' showing that he was regarded as the only impediment in the way of complete pro-slavery success. The balloting commenced May 1, the eighth day of the convention, it being still insisted that two-thirds of the whole convention, or 202 votes, were necessary to a choice, notwithstanding the withdrawals. The voting continued two days, during which there were fifty-seven ballotings. The lowest vote cast for Douglas upon any ballot was 147 and the highest 152½, while the remaining ballots were scattered among eight others. Upon the last Douglas received 151½, James Guthrie, of Kentucky, 65½ and 35 votes were scattering, upon which ballot Douglas would have been nominated but for the two-thirds rule. But this having been found to be, as Buchanan says, ''impossible,'' the convention adjourned to meet in Baltimore on June 18, 1860, with the recommendation that the vacancies occasioned by those who had withdrawn should be filled. The seceding delegates also held a convention of their own and adopted a platform of a general character, but specifically urging the acquisition of Cuba. They also adjourned to meet in Richmond, Va., on the second Monday in June, evidently expecting that as they had the support of Buchanan and his administration they would be able to bring to their side a majority of those from whom they had withdrawn, inasmuch as no such thing as the spirit of compromise existed. The country was obviously approaching an ominous and threatening crisis.

These seceders met in convention at Richmond as agreed upon, on June 11th, consisting of delegates from Alabama, Arkansas, Texas, Louisiana, Mississippi, Georgia, South Carolina, Florida, and one from each of the States of Tennessee and Virginia. After organization it adjourned to meet again on the 21st, so as to await the action of those who were to assemble at Baltimore on the 18th, with a view to negotiation. When the 18th arrived what was left of the Charleston Convention assembled in Baltimore. All the Northern States were fully represented, but the only delegates from the slave States were from Maryland, Virginia, Kentucky, Tennessee, North Carolina, and two from Delaware. The other slave States were not even called,—probably because they were taken at their word and their secession at Charleston considered complete and final. The convention, however, did not proceed far before there were other withdrawals from the slave-State delegations, leaving from 30 to 35 delegates to represent the entire South. But among these there remained enough of the enemies of Douglas to insist that he could not be regularly nominated for the Presidency without receiving two-thirds of the entire convention as it was when it first assembled at Charleston, that is, 202 votes. This, however, was treated as purely factious by the friends of Douglas, and he was nominated on the second ballot, having received 181 ½ votes with 13 scattering. Herschel V. Johnson, of Georgia, was placed upon the ticket with him as a candidate for Vice-President. As the South had resolved not to submit to this, but, if it occurred, to resist it, the seceders from that section again assembled—joined by 4 from California and 3 from Oregon—and by a unanimous vote nominated John C. Breckinridge of Kentucky, for President, and General Joseph Lane of Oregon, for Vice-President. They did not expect to elect this ticket, but intended by it, as was well understood, that under no possible condition of circumstances should Douglas ever be President. But there was an object beyond this, to accomplish which it was but an incident. A Constitutional Union Convention had met in Baltimore, May 9, 1860, and nominated John Bell of Tennessee, for President, and Edward Everett of Massachusetts for Vice-President, upon a platform stripped of all complications and pledged to "the Constitution of the country, the Union of the States, and the enforcement of the laws." And another National Convention had met at Chicago, May 16th, and nominated Abraham Lincoln of Illinois, for President, and Hannibal Hamlin of Maine, for Vice-President, upon a platform which declared that the right of each State "to order and control its own domestic institutions according to its own judgment exclusively" should be maintained,—that "the normal condition of all the territory of the United States is that of freedom,"—and that the Constitution does not "of its own force" carry slavery into any of these territories. To these two platforms the seceders were hostile —to the first because it proposed to cling to the Union as "the fathers" had formed it, and to the second because it refused to recognize every foot of the territory of the United States as slave territory. But to Douglas and the platform upon which he had been placed, they were more intensely hostile, for the reason, scarcely then concealed, that as Buchanan had under his administration allowed them to have their own way and they had availed themselves of his hesitation and prevarications to increase their power, they, with a kind of hallucination never yet explained or understood, chose to assume that Douglas and his multitude of friends were the seceders and not themselves. It is only necessary to examine carefully the proceedings of the conventions at Charleston, Richmond, and Baltimore, and to scrutinize the result of the Presidential election of that year to see all this. Douglas did not receive a single electoral vote from the whole of the slave States, except nine from Missouri, while Breckinridge received 72 and Bell 39, these last having been cast by Virginia, Tennessee and Kentucky. The total popular vote was 4,676,853, of which Lincoln received 1,806,352, Douglas 1,375,157, Breckinridge 845,763 and Bell 589,581. The plurality of Lincoln over Douglas was 491,159, or 5,710 less than Buchanan's over Fremont four years before, so that neither Lincoln nor Buchanan had a majority of the popular vote, although the former was elected President by 180 electoral votes or a majority of 57 of the whole.

The volume to which I have been referring plainly shows that Buchanan rejoiced at Douglas's defeat. He probably did not exult at the election of Lincoln, to which he contributed, in any other sense than as it crushed Douglas and his friends between "the upper and the nether millstone." His actual position, as he understood it, is easily explained—that as at the head of the 845,753, who represented the seceding faction at Charleston and Richmond and voted for Breckinridge, he felt himself entitled to rebuke and censure the 1,375,157 who voted for Douglas, because the latter, constituting a majority of more than half a million of the party first represented at Charleston, would not submit to the dictation of the minority. To them he attributed the defeat of Breckinridge in these strong condemnatory words: "It is clear that the original cause of the disaster was the persistent refusal of the friends of Mr. Douglas to recognize the constitutional rights of the slaveholding States in the Territories, established by the Supreme Court"—that is, the right of the slaveholders to carry their slaves to all the Territories and perpetuate their bondage. He cast aside all moderation, everything that had been hitherto considered conservative, and went to the extreme of vindicating the principles and policy of the 845,753 people of the South who had voted for Breckinridge and censuring and condemning the 3,181,-509 who had voted for Lincoln and Douglas, for upon this question he classed all these together. There never was before, in all our history, an instance where the voice of the people, legitimately and fairly expressed, was so utterly and flagrantly disregarded, nor any other where a President regarded it as one of the prerogatives of his office to pass a sentence of direct censure and rebuke upon the great body of the people. With strange infatuation he cut himself loose from a majority of those who had elected him President and set such an example of defiance to their will, as well as to that of the great body of the people of the United States, as to invite the extreme South to desperation. Then immediately followed preparations for war against the Union upon the part of those with whom he had co-operated and whose principles he had espoused. South Carolina passed an act calling a convention to prepare for seceding from the Union. Preparations looking to the same end were begun in other slave States. It was resolved that the triumph of the Southern minority over the Northern majority was of more value than the Union. Consequently his annual message was looked for with great anxiety, with the hope, on the part of the friends of the Union, that he would suggest some course of procedure that would arrest his extreme Southern allies and followers in the slave States and reconcile them to remain at peace with the Union. When the message appeared, however, December 3, 1860, it sent throughout the whole North and East and West a thrill almost of agony, which permeated all classes of society. Instead of suggesting some compromise, some peaceable plan of adjustment, he went to the full extent of censuring all who had voted for Lincoln and Douglas and justifying those who had voted for Breckinridge. To make both his censure and justification the more prominent he recommended that the Constitution should be so amended as to recognize the right of the Southern slaveholders to take their slaves into the Territories and hold them there in bondage. And, in addition, he declared that unless the Northern States should "repeal their unconstitutional and obnoxious enactments" regarding slavery, the South, "after having first used all peaceful and constitutional means to obtain redress, would be justified in revolutionary resistance to the government of the Union." He practiced no disguise upon this subject, and although he made a long and able argument to prove that secession was not a remedy contemplated by the Constitution, yet he furnished all the excuse the extreme South required, inasmuch as he classed secession and revolution together. And thus made bold by executive approval, the slaveholding States began to place themselves in hostile relations to the Union and to make preparations for open and military resistance to its authority.

South Carolina, taking the lead, passed an ordinance of secession December 20, 1860, and was followed during the month of January by other Southern States so rapidly that on February 4 a convention of their delegates met at Montgomery, Alabama, and formed a Southern Confederacy in open rebellion against the United States. Military preparations for aggressive war were immediately begun. The first question submitted to the Confederate Congress involved the propriety of attacking Fort Sumter and expelling the United States troops. Jefferson Davis, of Mississippi, was elected President, Alexander H. Stephens, of Georgia, Vice-President, and a full cabinet of executive officers was appointed. Important preparatory measures opening the way to these re-

25

sults had already been adopted. Possession had been obtained, by South Carolina, of Fort Moultrie and Castle Pinckney; the schooner William Aiken; the post-office and custom-house in Charleston; an arsenal at that place containing 70,000 stand of arms and other stores; the United States Steamer Marion, and the government vessel "Star of the West" had been fired upon. Georgia had seized Forts Pulaski and Jackson and the arsenal at Augusta containing two twelve-pound howitzers, two cannon, 22,000 muskets and rifles, and large stores of powder, ball and grape-shot; and had also seized several vessels belonging to citizens of New York. Florida had taken possession of the navy-yard at Tallahassee, and Forts Barrancas and McRae, also the arsenal at Chattahoochee, containing 500,000 rounds of musket cartridges, 300,000 rifle cartridges, and 50,000 pounds of gunpowder. Alabama had seized Fort Morgan containing 5,000 shot and shell, also Mt. Vernon Arsenal containing 20,000 stand of arms, 1,500 barrels, or 150,000 pounds, of powder, several pieces of cannon, a large quantity of munitions of war, and the revenue cutter Lewis Cass. Mississippi had seized the fort at Ship Island and the government hospital on the Mississippi river. Louisiana had seized Forts Jackson, St. Philip and Pike; the arsenal at Baton Rouge containing 50,000 small arms, 4 howitzers, 20 heavy pieces of ordnance, 2 batteries and 300 barrels of powder; all the quartermaster's and commissary stores in the State; the revenue cutter McClelland, and the Mint and Custom-house in New Orleans containing $593,303 in gold and silver. Texas had seized all the guns and stores on the steamship Texas; Forts

Chadbourne and Belknap; had received from General Twiggs all the stores under his command, estimated at $1,300,000, consisting of $55,000 in specie, 35,000 stand of arms, 26 pieces of mounted artillery, 44 dismounted, with ammunition, horses and wagons; and the revenue cutter Dodge, and Fort Brown. Arkansas had seized the arsenal at Little Rock containing 9,000 small arms, 40 cannon and a large amount of ammunition. North Carolina had seized Forts Johnson and Caswell. And, in fact, there was nothing belonging to the United States within the boundaries of the seceded States that was not taken possession of by them, for the express and avowed purpose of putting an end to the authority of the United States within those boundaries by aggressive war.

These things were all done during the administration of Buchanan, and were not only preparations for war, but actual and existing war. It does not require the actual firing of guns to make a state of war; but if it did, the firing upon the Star of the West, in Charleston harbor, January 9, 1861, while Buchanan was yet President, could not be made to signify anything less than war. But preparations for assault—either of a nation or an individual—are sufficient to justify the threatened party in doing whatever is demanded by the law of self-defense. The civil war, therefore, broke out under Buchanan's administration, and imposed upon him the patriotic obligation of defending, with all the power at his executive command, the integrity of the Union. Any other President would have done so promptly and energetically; especially would Jackson have done so, without a moment's hesitation. But he hesitated and temporized, and talked learnedly about the constitutional power of coercing a State, while the enemies of the Union were, in plain view, undermining the pillars upon which it rested,—imitating Nero who "fiddled while Rome was burning." Instead of defying all adversaries of the government—as Jackson would have done—he received envoys, or commissioners from the Confederate authorities, admitted them to the Presidential mansion, and suffered them to declare that the Union had failed to answer the ends of its creation, and to treat of it, in his presence, as a thing of the past. At this point, he seemed to have been awakened, for the first time, to the actual reality of himself and his administration—to have realized that his prevarication and timidity had well-nigh cost the nation its life. How he must have felt then when aroused from his dream is more easily conceived than explained. But it was too late. He did not desire to see the Union destroyed, but having acquiesced so long in a course of measures planned for that purpose alone, he found his executive hands tied so tightly that he could not unloose them. Probably he then repented —as I am willing to suppose he did, and as his refusal to remove the United States troops from Sumter back to Moultrie indicated,—but whether he did or not, he had gone so far and was so completely circumvented by those whose cause he had espoused in the recent Presidential election, that there was nothing left for him to do but to turn the government over to his successor in a state of civil war!

Your friend as ever
A. Lincoln

CHAPTER XVI

ABRAHAM LINCOLN

IF I were to consult alone my personal inclinations, I should occupy a considerable space in expressing my estimate of the leading characteristics and virtues of Lincoln. But I do not deem it advisable to unduly tax in this way the patience of any reader into whose hands this sketch may chance to fall, because his life and history are universally known throughout the whole country and among all classes and conditions of people. Genius has taxed its best energies in the search after glowing eulogiums upon his name; and the popular affection for him will endure far beyond the time when the few who have cast aspersions upon him shall be forgotten. My attachment for him was very strong—exceeding mere ordinary respect. I practiced law in some of the courts of Illinois he had been in the habit of attending, and from his and my own professional associates had learned his estimable qualities before I had ever seen him. We met for the first time in the Thirtieth Congress, during which we served together in the House of Representatives. Several circumstances conspired to bring us together as if we had been old friends and acquaintances. Our homes were not very far apart,—the interests of our constituents were identical,—we had the same party attachments,—and there were but about three months difference in our ages, he having been that much my senior. Consequently, there speedily grew up between us such close and intimate relations as only exist among those whose sympathies are in unison. These relations were never disturbed, although he knew I did not always agree with him concerning the details of his administrative policy. The nobility and generosity of his nature were too well grounded to permit mere differences of opinion to interfere with his friendship. In this respect he was an admirable model for imitation, and if his example had been more generally followed, many of the evils which have afflicted the country would undoubtedly have been avoided.

The nomination of Lincoln for the Presidency was a triumph of conservatism, which he distinctly and emphatically represented. His principal competitors were William H. Seward and Salmon P. Chase, both of whom were men of distinguished ability and better known throughout the nation than he was, but they were the representatives of extreme views upon the slavery question, the former having expressed the idea of an "irrepressible conflict" between the sections, and the latter, if he did not approve it, having gone to a like extreme. The convention which nominated him assembled in Chicago, May 16, 1860, and was composed of 465 delegates, representing all the free States and the following slave States: Delaware, Maryland, Virginia, Kentucky, Missouri and Texas. Before the balloting began a platform was adopted containing this emphatic pledge: "That the maintenance inviolate of the rights of the

States, and especially the right of each State, to order and control its own domestic institutions according to its own judgment exclusively, is essential to that balance of power on which the perfection and endurance of our political fabric depends.'' This was understood to mean, and did expressly mean, that the right of each State to establish slavery or to maintain it where it already existed, was guaranteed by the Constitution. Upon this point there was nothing equivocal. Nor was there with regard to ''the new dogma'' set up by the politicians of the slave States, whereby it was claimed that ''the Constitution, of its own force, carries slavery into any or all of the Territories of the United States,'' which proposition it denied as ''a dangerous political heresy,'' and avowed this counter theory, ''that the normal condition of all the territory of the United States is that of freedom.''

The fact should not be disguised, however, that there were among the supporters of Lincoln some who represented more extreme anti-slavery sentiments than were set forth in this platform, and who would have been more content with a candidate reflecting Northern in opposition to Southern sectionalism. But, at the same time, it should not be forgotten that they constituted a disturbing element in the convention itself, and brought about a controversy in that body between themselves and the conservative members, and that the latter triumphed over them by securing a large majority in favor of the platform, and the unanimous nomination of Lincoln as the representative of its principles. The pretense, therefore, which was afterwards set up, that Lincoln was an

entirely sectional candidate, was answered and overthrown
by the palpable fact that the convention announced these
three distinctively conservative propositions: 1. That no
power existed in the National Government to interfere with
slavery in the States, but that the States themselves could
introduce, maintain or abolish it at their own pleasure. 2.
That the Constitution did not, of its own force, carry slavery into the Territories. 3. That the normal condition of
the Territories was that of freedom. To have said, as the
slavery extensionists did, that this was sectionalism was
in direct conflict with the expressed opinions of all the
departments of the government—legislative, executive
and judicial—frequently repeated during all the previous
life of the nation, especially by the ordinance for the government of the Northwestern Territory, the Missouri
Compromise, and the compromise of 1850.

It should be remembered, also, that there were differences between the opponents of Lincoln as irreconcilable
as those existing among his supporters, and far more sectional. We have already seen that they disrupted the
Charleston convention, and could not be reconciled at
that of Baltimore; and more than that, their disruption
led to the nomination of Douglas by the latter convention, and that of Breckinridge by the seceders in another
purely sectional assemblage at Richmond. The platform
of these seceders made a distinctive issue by affirming
that the Constitution carried slavery into the Territories,
but as this was denied both by the convention which
nominated Lincoln and that which nominated Douglas,
Breckinridge was made the representative of a mere sectional faction, making no pretense whatever to national-

ity. Of course those engaged in this movement did not expect his election, and consequently could have but one object in view, that is, to assure the defeat of Douglas, in order that, by the election of Lincoln, the slave States should become so consolidated as to be prepared for any future exigency. There was not a man concerned in it who did not know that the proposition that the Constitution carried slavery into the Territories represented the extremest Southern sectionalism, and that the North would never consent to it.

In 1850, while the Senate had under consideration the measures which became the compromise of that year, Jeff Davis, of Mississippi, moved an amendment substantially affirming this proposition by declaring void all laws which prevented slave-owners from transporting their slaves into the Territories and holding them there as such. The Senate rejected this amendment by a vote of 33 against it to 22 in its favor. The affirmative vote was entirely sectional, every Senator being from a slave State, while the negative was composed of all the Senators from the free States, and Benton, of Missouri; Clay, of Kentucky; Foote, of Mississippi; Pierce, of Maryland, and Spruance and Wales, of Delaware—making six from the slave States. There never occurred after this any reason to believe that the proposition would ever meet with more favor, and being so contrary to the principles established by "the fathers" during all the early history of the government, the conclusion can not be escaped that the friends of Breckinridge were rallied to its support for the express purpose, already formed,

of making it—knowing it would be rejected by the country—the rallying point for the inauguration of a war of
the slave States against the Union. It was a flagrant
false pretense, bottomed upon a treasonable design.

The result of the election was the expression of public
confidence in the conservatism of Lincoln. Upon the
three most prominent questions—the right of Congress to
interfere with slavery in the States, the normal condition
of freedom in the Territories, and the constitutional obligation to execute the fugitive slave law—he and Douglas
were agreed. This is shown by their great debate in Illinois, which, at the time, attracted universal attention.
Upon the first two of these propositions Lincoln was always express and emphatic, representing therein not only
his own opinions but those of the convention which nominated him. In his reply to Douglas, when their joint
debate was brought to a close at Alton, October 15, 1858,
he dwelt at some length upon the last, the fugitive slave
law, and said that, while he had no taste for catching
slaves when they escaped into the free States, yet as the
right to recapture them was guaranteed by the Constitution to their masters, he gave his support to a fugitive
slave law because it was provided for by the Constitution. At this point of his argument he insisted that
Douglas was an abolitionist, because, if his "squatter
sovereignty" doctrine, which gave the people of a Territory the right to create or abolish slavery, were sustained,
then a Territorial Legislature would have the power to
override this constitutional provision by abolishing slavery
and making fugitive slaves free! This must have stag-
gered Douglas not a little, as it was undoubtedly a home-

thrust, and although he alluded to it in his reply, it was jocularly done, but he made no attempt at an answer or an explanation.

Lincoln's conservatism was distinctly expressed in a speech made by him in September, 1859, at Cincinnati, wherein, touching slavery, he declared: "I say that we must not interfere with the institution of slavery in the States where it exists, because the Constitution forbids it, and the general welfare does not require us to do so. We must not withhold an efficient fugitive slave law because the Constitution requires us, as I understand it, not to withhold such a law. But we must prevent the outspreading of the institution, because neither the Constitution nor general welfare requires us to extend it. We must prevent the revival of the African slave-trade and the enacting by Congress of a Territorial slave code. We must prevent each of these things being done by either congresses or courts. The people of these United States are the rightful masters of both congresses and courts, not to overthrow the Constitution, but to overthrow the men who pervert the Constitution."

It will be seen, therefore, that his chief and controlling object was to prevent the extension of slavery into the Territories and the consequent increase of the slave power. He knew—as everybody else did—that the object of the slave States was to re-acquire the political power which they had lost by the rapid growth of the free States, so that they could have absolute control of all national affairs—including executive, legislative, and judiciary—and make the free States dependent upon them. He was unwilling to arrest the growth and development of the country by converting free into slave territory—well knowing the blasting and blighting influences of slavery wherever it had existed. Consequently, when the result of the Presidential contest of 1860 is properly viewed, it will be seen—now that the passions then prevailing have subsided—that the only question settled adversely to the South, by Lincoln's election, was the non-extension of slavery into the Territories; in other words, the refusal of the North to turn over to the South the entire management of national affairs. It is impossible fairly to reach any other conclusion than this, when the positions of the several candidates and the votes received by each of them are properly considered. There were 4,676,853 popular votes cast. Lincoln received 1,866,352; Douglas, 1,375,157; Breckinridge, 845,763, and Bell, 589,581. Lincoln's plurality over Douglas was 491,195. The majorities and pluralities in the States were such that the electoral vote was divided as follows: Lincoln 180, Breckinridge 72, Bell 39, Douglas 12; which gave Douglas 60 electoral votes fewer than Breckinridge, nothwithstanding the popular vote of the former was 529,394 more than that of the latter. But the vote of Breckinridge was almost entirely sectional, inasmuch as he was supported by all the slave States except Kentucky, Tennessee, and Virginia, which voted for Bell, and Missouri, which voted for Douglas,— this being the only slave State that did so. It is impossible to conceive of a more sectional vote than that cast for Breckinridge. It was intended as the condemnation of both Lincoln and Douglas and an arraignment of the entire North, for the single reason that the people in that section would not assent to the new and strange proposition that the Constitution by its own terms carried slavery into all the Territories,—the most ultra latitudinarian construction of that instrument ever before known, and which threw the old Federalist doctrine of implied powers entirely in the shade. I once heard the question discussed by Webster and Calhoun in the Senate, and was never more forcibly impressed by the difference between a profound constitutional lawyer and statesman, and one who had "cabined, cribbed, confined," the faculties of his great intellect within the narrow confines of sectional fanaticism. Webster's argument was clear, comprehensive and conclusive, and so brushed away the sophistries of Calhoun as to make the latter appear feebler than he would have been if not hampered by sectional prejudice. The one defended the great principle of nationality, for the preservation and perpetuity of the Constitution was expressly extended over the original thirteen States; while the latter placed such limitations upon that principle, and so hedged it in, as to make it subordinate to the higher and broader powers of the States, as distinct and independent sovereignties. Webster considered the Constitution as a sacred and indissoluble contract of union between all the people of the United States; Calhoun regarded it as expressing merely a confederation of independent States, each one of which could judge for itself of infractions upon it, and terminate the Union at its own pleasure, in defiance of all national and coercive power.

When the Presidential election occurred, in November, 1860, it was impossible to anticipate the consequences likely to ensue between that time and the commencement of Lincoln's administration, March 4, 1861. No man was ever elected President with such threatening and uncertain surroundings as Lincoln. The condition of affairs had never before been so agitated. All who observed intelligently the progress of events could see a cloud appearing upon the national sky, which, if not then "larger than a man's hand," exhibited unmistakable evidences of increasing dimensions. A dissolution of the Union had been threatened in the event of his election, and there were such evidences of passion and anger among the Southern people as to excite in the minds of those familiar with them the fear, if not apprehension, that these threats were not mere idle bravado. The Northern people were in a condition of quietude in striking contrast with these warlike threats, and hence the preparations for war among the agitators of the South,—as detailed in the last chapter,—were made almost without observation even in some portions of the South, and without knowledge or suspicion in the North. By the secret methods adopted a state of war against the Union was actually produced during Buchanan's administration, and the government, consequently, was passed over to Lincoln in that condition as an inheritance from his immediate predecessor. Consequently Lincoln was in no sense chargeable with the seizure of the forts, arms and ammunition in the South by the enemies of the Union, because this had been accomplished under Buchanan, who must have known it unless neglectful of official duty, or if he did know it, was almost *particeps criminis* in not resisting it by requiring the forts to be re-surrendered and the

arms and ammunition returned. It must therefore remain as a historic fact that Lincoln was not responsible
for the condition of affairs when his administration commenced.

I have stated elsewhere, and it deserves to be repeated, that firing of guns or actual bloodshed is not necessary to create a state of war. Nor is war always made
by public proclamation. A country or State threatened
with hostile invasion is not required to await an attack
from the invaders, but may justifiably open fire upon
them in self-defense whenever they begin their military
preparations. These facts are incontrovertible: That
the authority of the Union was defied and rebellion
against it was begun by South Carolina as early as
December 20, 1860,—a few weeks only after Lincoln's
election; that the same was done by other Southern
States during January, 1861, and that within the next
month these rebellious movements culminated in the formation and organization of what was called the Confederate Government—in flagrant opposition to that of the
United States—with Jeff Davis as its President. And to
assure reasonable prospect of success in these rebellious
measures, the forts, arsenals, arms and ammunition belonging to the United States were seized with hostile in-
tent, as detailed in the last chapter. Moreover, the Star
of the West—a government boat—was fired upon in
Charleston harbor. If all these things did not create a
state of war against the Union it would be difficult to
conceive a condition of things that would do so. The
Confederates themselves regarded war as existing, and
boasted that they had achieved their independence with-

out bloodshed. They interpreted the silence and non-
resistance of Buchanan to mean acquiescence upon the
part of the United States government; and, with an unparalleled degree of infatuation, sent ambassadors or envoys—after the custom of separate and independent nations—to demand from him that the United States troops
should be removed from Fort Sumter and that strong-
hold be turned over to them!

It would be hard to convey to the mind of one not already informed the degree of responsibility which rested
upon Lincoln when, with these surroundings, the government passed out of Buchanan's hands into his. No
President ever passed through the inaugural ceremonies
under such trying circumstances. He could not fail to
see, rapidly multiplying in every direction, sources of
embarrassment which none of his predecessors had ever
encountered. He inherited a problem which Buchanan
could not solve, and which, if he did not solve, would
signify to mankind that the life of the nation had ex-
pired and that thereafter for all time the belief in man's
capacity for self-government would be mere delusion. If
he had indulged in imaginings he could have fancied that
he heard the shouts of imperialism at the victory it had
partially won over popular institutions, and if he had
not been a man of indomitable courage despair would
have expelled the last vestige of hope from his heart.
How different his position from that of Buchanan! The
latter, doubtless, experienced a sense of gratification at
the thought that the tremendous load of official responsibility, heaped upon him by those who had elected him
to the Presidency, was removed from his own shoulders

to those of his successor, and that if Lincoln were crushed beneath its weight he could look out from his retreat at Wheatland and exult, along with his Southern friends, at Lincoln's ignominious downfall; not that he desired the Union to be destroyed, but that he looked upon the Southern Confederacy as the mere means to an end—that is, the acquisition of such political power by its allies as would enable them thereafter to manage the government of the United States in their own way and for the accomplishment of their own objects. It may not stretch the imagination overmuch to suppose him influenced by the desire that no more fresh blood from the Western prairies should course through Presidential veins, but that the country should be restored to the chivalric dominion of the slave oligarchy, to whom he was himself indebted for the Presidential office. However this may have been, the beginning of Lincoln's administration was distinguished by far greater fidelity to the Union than the closing period of Buchanan's. Let the searcher after truth read well the history of those times, and he will see this as plainly as the sun at noonday when the sky is without a cloud. And if he will read the inaugural address of Lincoln he can not withhold encomiums upon the sublime grandeur with which he rose above the mere atmosphere of party and expressed his fidelity alone to the Constitution and an unbroken Union. No undue harshness or censure was mingled with his eloquent words, but almost every thought expressed embodied within it a fervid appeal to the patriotism of the whole country, the South as well as the North. Instead of making it an indictment, with exasperating counts charging treason and

26

rebellion, against those who had vainly supposed they
had dissolved the Union and set up a rival and independent government of their own, he invoked the spirit of
national concord and harmony, intending it to be understood that he considered the Union still undissolved. To
the deluded and misguided South he declared that, under his administration, all the rights of the slave States
over their slave property should be preserved inviolate
and that the fugitive slave law should be executed in
strict conformity to the guarantees of the Constitution.
With regard to the demand that the Constitution carried
slavery into the Territories by its own terms, he merely
re-avowed what he and Douglas and Bell had all affirmed
during the Presidential canvass and which had been sustained by the enormous popular vote of 3,831,090 unit-
edly cast for them, against the meager minority of 589,-
581 cast for Breckinridge.

Having thus shown to the country and the world that
this constituted the only ground which those who were
endeavoring to destroy the government had left to them,
he became patriotically inspired by a proper sense of his
own responsibilities and declared that, in his opinion,
"no State, upon its own mere motion, can lawfully get
out of the Union; that resolves and ordinances to that
effect are legally void; and that acts of violence within
any State or States, against the authority of the United
States, are insurrectionary, or revolutionary, according
to circumstances." And having laid down these incon-
testably correct national propositions, he followed them
immediately by further declaring: "I, therefore, consider that, in view of the Constitution and the laws, the

Union is unbroken, and to the extent of my ability I shall take care, as the Constitution itself expressly enjoins upon me, that the laws of the Union be faithfully executed in all the States." And he then proceeded to say that, "there need be no bloodshed or violence; and there shall be none unless it be forced upon the national authority," but that, whatever the future should reveal, the Union should be preserved in its integrity, and the laws be executed to its extremest borders. There was no threatening, no bravado, or bluster, but a plain, distinct, and explicit announcement of his purpose, to protect, defend and maintain the National Government as intact as it was when it came from the hands of its founders. To his "countrymen, one and all," North and South, he made an earnest appeal, urging them to "think calmly and well" upon the advantages they had derived from "the old Constitution unimpaired." With his heart stirred by patriotic emotions he addressed himself directly to the organized enemies of the Union, in these words: "You can have no conflict without being yourselves the aggressors. You have no oath registered in heaven to destroy the government; while I have the most solemn one to 'preserve, defend, and protect' it." And as if further inspired by the hope, if not the belief, that they might yet be turned away from their rebellious course, he still further admonished them in these beautiful and pathetic words, which yet quicken the palpitation of every patriot heart: "We are not enemies, but friends. We must not be enemies. Though passion may have strained, it must not break our bonds of affection. The mystic cord of memory, stretching from every

battle-field and patriot grave to every living heart and
hearthstone all over this broad land, will yet swell the
chorus of the Union, when again touched, as surely they
will be, by the better angels of our natures.''

Lincoln passionately loved the Union, and was unwilling to leave undone whatever, as President, he had the
rightful authority to do, to convince its enemies of their
disloyalty to it. He gave them full time for deliberation before resorting to harsh measures for retaking the
forts, arsenals, guns and ammunition, which were the
property of the United States and which they had un-
lawfully seized. In this he acted according to the
promptings of his own generous nature, and was undoubtedly stimulated by the hope that his appeal to their
reason and patriotism would not be unavailing. If any
man ever acted under the dictation of kindly emotions he
did under the circumstances here detailed, and if he had
left no other evidences of his fitness for the Presidential
office, they were abundantly sufficient to attest it. As
there had yet been no blood shed, although a state of
war existed and actual military operations were threatened, he flattered himself with the desire and hope
that these calamities might be avoided and the direful
consequences of civil war escaped, if there were yet left
a single spark of patriotism in the hearts of the Southern
people. And thus he became, at this important period of
his administration, one of the grandest figures in modern
American history—rising up to the loftiest altitude of
statesmanship.

The peaceful overtures of Lincoln were met with scorn
by the Southern leaders, who, already maddened by the

steps they had previously taken, were stimulated by their passions to still greater acts of folly. Within ten days of the inaugural, and in the very face of its frank avowals and earnest appeal, two commissioners, who pretended to represent an independent government of seven States which had withdrawn from the Union, appeared in Washington City and solicited an official interview with the Secretary of State. Their avowed object was to adjust by negotiation with the administration the relations thereafter to subsist between the two governments—that is, the old Union and the Southern Confederacy. Even this bold and flagrant act of disloyalty—unparalleled in impudence—did not disturb the equanimity of Lincoln; and he simply caused these commissioners to be notified by the Secretary of State that he did not consider the Union dissolved, but that the seven States which had assumed to themselves the power to dissolve it were still members of it and would be so regarded by him. There were no threats of violence accompanying this announcement,— nothing vituperative. On the other hand, it was but the repetition of the firm and resolute purpose he had expressed in his inaugural to maintain an unbroken Union. The communication to this effect was delivered to these pretended commissioners April 8, 1861, and immediately communicated to those who had appointed them, who availed themselves of its receipt to inflame still more the passions of their followers. The effect produced was precisely what they desired, for on the third day thereafter—April 11—the United States officer in command of Fort Sumter had made upon him a formal demand for the surrender of that fort to the ''Confederate States.''

This he declined, and was thereupon notified the next morning, April 12, that General Beauregard would open "the fire of his batteries" on the fort in one hour thereafter. This threat was carried into execution and the fight continued for thirty-four hours, when the quarters of the fort were entirely burnt, the main gates destroyed by fire, the walls seriously injured, the magazine surrounded by flames; whereupon, after the ammunition and provisions were almost entirely exhausted, the fort was surrendered into the hands of the Confederates, who took possession of it on April 14, 1861. And thus the state of war which had previously existed was changed into actual war—the most destructive civil war of modern times. Lincoln did nothing to bring it on, but everything within his power to prevent it. It was the work, solely and entirely, of those misguided men who had persuaded themselves to believe, with strange infatuation, that Lincoln was an imbecile,—that the Northern people were social mud-sills, incapable of ever becoming soldiers,—and that they then had it in their power to pull down and destroy the grandest structure of civil government ever erected in the world. They were crazed by the firing of their own guns and the conquest of Sumter. Previous to that time they had professed to be only acting in self-defense, merely to repel the invasion of the South by the armies of the Union. But when Sumter fell into their hands so easily, they roused themselves up by their own shouts of rejoicing to such an extreme of hallucination as openly to avow the ultimate purpose of taking possession of Washington City, indignantly hurling Lincoln from the Presidential chair, floating their flag from the dome of the National Capitol, and ultimately over Faneuil Hall in Boston! While salvos of artillery were sounding in their streets and reason had been driven from her throne, their usurping Secretary of War publicly made these treasonable boasts, and they were responded to throughout the South, especially by the newspapers. Among these, the Richmond *Enquirer* was in hot haste to say, the day after the affair at Sumter: "Nothing is more probable than that President Davis will soon march an army through North Carolina and Virginia to Washington;" and the New Orleans *Picayune*—about a week after— boastingly avowed that "the first fruits" of the rebellion would be "the removal of Lincoln and his cabinet and whatever he can carry away, to the safer neighborhood of Harrisburg or Cincinnati—perhaps to Buffalo or Cleveland."

It should not be forgotten that when these things occurred and these threats were made, there had not been a single man mustered nor a single gun furnished nor a single pound of powder issued by the United States for attack upon the rebellious authorities of any Southern State or any military preparations made for that purpose. When Lincoln became assured by the capture of Sumter that his appeal to Southern patriotism was entirely unheeded he could wait no longer, and on April 15, three days after Sumter had fallen, he issued his proclamation calling for 75,000 of the militia of the States to enable him to execute the laws, and called an extra session of Congress to meet July 4, 1861. Until then he had made no threats nor any hostile demonstrations against the South, but had appealed to the people there to cease their hostility to the Union and obey the Constitution. It is no part of my purpose to treat of the military events which followed, for, besides being necessary parts of our national history, they are still recounted at thousands of our firesides by the gallant men who participated in them, many of whom testify by their wounds and shattered health the desperate character of the deadly conflict. And throughout the South there are multitudes of little hillocks which remind the survivors that husbands, fathers, brothers and sons gave up their lives for the "lost cause." How many of these—if they could speak from their tombs—would testify to the injustice of the cause for which they sacrificed their lives it is not given to any of us to know; but this we do know, without the least peradventure, that the Southern people were deceived and misled by those who assumed to be their leaders and superiors, and that instead of the final victorious triumph they were promised, their folly was rewarded by defeat and desolation. They went to war, not to resist interference with slavery in the States, for nothing of that kind was either threatened or contemplated, but for the sole right of maintaining such an interpretation of the Constitution as would allow them to transplant slavery in the Territories. Slaveholders demanded this and enticed non-slaveholders into the net dexterously woven by them, so that the latter became the best "fighting material" of the rebellious army. And the price they paid, in addition to the loss of thousands of brave men and millions of money, besides the humiliation of defeat, was the loss of all their slaves, every one of whom

was set free forever. How this was done by a few strokes
of Lincoln's executive pen is easily told.

Lincoln, in the spirit of fairness which characterized
his official conduct, on March 6, 1862—when the war
had been in progress nearly a year—addressed a communication to Congress wherein he proposed that the
States should be invited to free their slaves upon the condition that the United States should pay them a sufficient
amount of money to compensate for their loss. This he
considered justifiable under the Constitution as a war
measure, and upon the score of economy as less expen-
sive than the prosecution of the war; and his reasons
having been approved by both Houses of Congress,
efforts were made to carry his proposed plan into effect.
A good deal was done in the border slave States looking
to that end, but nothing was practically accomplished,
and the war continued. Nevertheless, the proposition
was creditable to Lincoln, because it displayed, not only
his regret at the existence of civil war, but his ardent
desire to bring it to an end and to remove entirely the
cause of strife between the sections, because none knew
better than he that slavery was the sole cause of the war.
Opposition to this scheme came from two sources—the
distinctive abolitionists, who were unwilling to recognize
human beings as slaves, and the slaveholders themselves,
except a few who were liberal-minded and patriotic. Not
disconcerted, however, by this failure, and with all his
energies devoted to the restoration of peace, he, on September 22, 1862, issued a proclamation wherein he declared that he would lay before Congress at its next ses-

sion this same proposition for compensated emancipation. But in this same document he notified all who were the owners of slaves in any of the States that their slaves would be set free on January 1, 1863, if upon that day the States in which they resided were in rebellion against the United States. This gave full three months' notice to the rebellious States of the condition upon which they had it in their power to save their slave property—the simple condition being that they should lay down their arms and revive their allegiance to the United States. This they refused, as everybody knows, so that when January 1, 1863, arrived, he issued another proclamation declaring that in the rebellious States "all persons held as slaves" shall thenceforth be "forever free."

The war continued—increasing, if possible, in violence and destructiveness. The conciliatory and conservative course of Lincoln contributed more to intensify than to lessen the passions of the South. The rebel troops pressed forward towards the North—finding nothing to impede them in the sympathizing South. They approached the National Capitol so nearly that the roar of the cannon at Bull's Run was heard in Washington City. Everywhere the excitement had become so intense that it could not have been surpassed. But Lincoln was calm and composed. His courage never failed. On the contrary, it rose with the occasion, and every message from the fields of blood and strife gave birth to increased energy and fresh resolutions to maintain the life of the nation and the integrity of the Union. In a private conversation with him, a few days after the battle of Bull's Run, we discussed the existing condition of affairs. He had a map before him, upon the table, with his finger resting upon the point occupied by the rebel forces, and the question we were considering was how they were to be driven back. Neither of us was familiar with the strategies of war—the marches and counter-marches of contending armies,—but I shall never forget his appearance when, with his flashing eyes intently gazing into mine, he exclaimed with intense animation: "The rebels shall never cross the Potomac river, or if they do it must be done over my dead body; for the eternal hills shall fly 'from their firm base as soon as I!' " Before I left him he added, in moderated tones: "It will all come right. The government will stand and the Union be preserved, in spite of all the powers that can conspire against them. The heart of the nation beats patriotically. God is upon our side, and will stimulate the courage and strengthen the arms of 'the boys in blue.' Mark what I say, it will all come right."

And it did come right in so far as a flagrant wrong can ever do so. He was mistaken, however, in supposing that the rebel forces would never cross the Potomac,— his mind, at the time here referred to, having manifestly been directed to their attempt to capture Washington City. They did afterwards succeed in crossing into Maryland at Harper's Ferry and in concentrating in large numbers at Gettysburg, in Pennsylvania, from which point after their defeat in one of the brilliant battles of the war they ultimately returned into Virginia, where, with General Lee in the chief command, their army was drawn together at Richmond, Petersburg, and intermediate points. Here the end was reached. The hard blows of Grant could be withstood no longer.   Lincoln's prediction was fulfilled:—God was upon our side, and "the boys in blue" were invincible.   Then came the period of "reconstruction," and that, too, has been completed; and we now present to the world a Union which has survived the shock of the fiercest war of modern times,—is bound fast together by the sentiment of a common nationality,—and is stretched out from ocean to ocean, with not one broken link in the chain which binds the States together and holds more than sixty millions of people in fraternal unity.   The light which madness and folly attempted to extinguish is growing brighter and brighter every day,—flashing forth to all the nations and peoples of the earth from whom the blessings of Christian civilization have not been withheld.   To us, therefore, who have survived the terrible crisis of civil war, and to the generation since born—both in the North and in the South—the lesson taught by the rebellion should not be lost, so that the patriotic sentiment of Jackson may sink deeply and abide in every American heart, "the Union forever, one and inseparable."

Lincoln's method of conducting the war and the conservatism of his policy—even to the extent of his emancipation proclamation—were approved by the loyal people with extraordinary unanimity.   Before the termination of the conflict, and when the deepest anxiety pervaded all the circles of society, a nominating convention met at Baltimore, June 7, 1864, to select his successor, by which, after adopting a platform indorsing his policy and earnestly maintaining the Union, he was unanimously renominated, together with Andrew Johnson, of Tennes-

see, as a candidate for the Vice-Presidency. In opposition to these nominations another convention was held in
Chicago, August 29, 1864, by which it was declared
"that after four years of failure to restore the Union by
the experiment of war," the time had arrived which demanded "that immediate efforts be made for a cessa-
tion of hostilities," and the questions then made, by the
South, dependent upon the issue of war, should be submitted to a National Convention. By this body General
George B. McClellan was nominated for the Presidency,
and George H. Pendleton for the Vice-Presidency.
Thus the issue was distinct and emphatic—whether the
war should be abandoned as a "failure" or fought out
to the bitter end. The result was, that in the 25 States
that voted—11 not voting—the aggregate popular vote
was 4,024,792, of which Lincoln received 2,216,067,
and McClellan 1,808,725,—this giving to the former a
majority of 407,342 over the latter, who received majorities in only three States, Delaware, Kentucky, and
New Jersey. The electoral votes cast were 212 for Lincoln, and 21 for McClellan. In his second inaugural,
delivered March 4, 1865, Lincoln exhibited no signs of
quaking nerves, but expressed a resolute determination
to carry on the war, although he accompanied this declaration with the fond hope and fervent prayer to God that
the "mighty scourge of war may speedily pass away."
And he closed with these pathetic and eloquent words:
"With malice towards none, with charity for all, with
firmness in the right as God gives us to see the right, let
us finish the work we are in, to bind up the nation's
wounds, to care for him who shall have borne the battle,

and for his widow and his orphans, to do all which may achieve and cherish a just and a lasting peace among ourselves and with all nations.''

The re-election of Lincoln, together with his stirring words and resoluteness of purpose,—indicating, as they did, the most unfaltering courage—had, doubtless, much to do with the surrender of Lee, and the consequent collapse of the rebellion. That event occurred April 9, 1865,—a little over a month after the inaugural—and with it the great conflict came to an end, the indissolubility of the Union was established, and its integrity vindicated. All patriotic hearts bounded with joy, and wherever throughout the North men, women or children were gathered together each congratulated the other that the end of fratricidal strife was near. Sorrow for the afflicted South—its deserted hearthstones, agonized and lacerated hearts, and desolated fields, took the place of revenge, and there was not a single heart in all the land more filled with sympathy than that of the generous-minded Lincoln. He was at the headquarters of Grant when that great soldier was encircling the forces of Lee, as the anaconda winds itself around its victims, and before he left for the capital clearly foresaw that the proud and rebellious spirit of the South was broken. After he reached Washington City an immense crowd assembled in front of the executive mansion, and then for the first time since his first inauguration he was enabled to say to them that they met ''not in sorrow, but in gladness of heart,'' and to promise that he would proclaim '' a national thanksgiving.'' With most becoming modesty he referred to himself, seeming to have forgotten his own participation in the cause of the Union, while his heart overran with gratitude to the gallant men who had borne the " harder part " upon the march, in the camp, and upon the fields of battle. Of these he said: " Their honors must not be parceled out with others. I, myself, was near the front, and had the pleasure of transmitting much of the good news to you. But no part of the honor for plan or execution is mine. To General Grant, his skillful officers, and brave men, all belongs." He never spoke afterwards in public. On the evening of April 14, 1865,—less than six weeks after his second in-auguration, and on the third day after these last public utterances—the felonious and traitorous bullet of the assassin terminated his earthly career. Everybody is familiar with the story of that sad event,—it has been learned by the children from their school-books, and re-peated in melancholy tones at thousands of firesides. It stands out so prominently among the most heinous crimes of the age that the death of the assassin does not atone for it. The deep-seated melancholy which it oc-casioned attested the high estimation in which he was held by patriotic people everywhere, and among them the sentiment was universal that he

" Hath borne his faculties so meek, hath been
So clear in his great office, that his virtues
Will plead like angels, trumpet-tongued, against
The deep damnation of his taking off."

So much has been said, written and published illustra-tive of the life and character of Lincoln, both public and private, as to render any additional reflections of mine

unnecessary. Besides, in what has been here said, I
have had other objects in view, the chief of which has
been to show that, upon the score of services to the
Union cause, there were none who surpassed him or who
served that cause from purer, more disinterested or more
unselfish motives. Judged of by the events which were
crowded into the four years of his Presidential service,
he stands out prominently to the public view as one of
the most conspicuous figures of modern times. His
name will continue to adorn the pages of American history so long as the Union shall exist, and if there shall
ever come a time when it does not, even then it will incite the admiration of all who venerate integrity of purpose and those high qualities of head and heart which
make their possessors fit examples for imitation. Not
one of the twenty-one Presidents I have seen and known,
in my opinion, surpassed him in those attributes of character which were developed by him during the perilous
course of his administration. From the beginning to
the end he never flinched or exhibited the least signs of
indecision or wavering. Nor did he ever doubt the final
result. Accordingly, if misfortunes befell any portion of
the Union army or their columns were broken by the enemy, his hope and expectation of final triumph never
forsook him. His courage was never shaken and im-
parted its influence to others, so that there, perhaps, was
not an instance where those who had intercourse with him
did not have their patriotism refreshed and strengthened.
I have known instances of that kind, and there were
doubtless many others, which combined to prove that he
possessed a personality so strikingly marked as to do

much towards molding and directing public sentiment, by this means serving the cause of the Union.

Lincoln was plain and simple in his manner. There was not the least pride or ostentation about him. He possessed a high appreciation of those who made themselves worthy of his confidence by meritorious conduct, while the rules sometimes prescribed for the creation of ranks and orders in social intercourse were unknown to him. He measured men by their worth, not their pretentions—by their conduct, not their mere professions. While he was sometimes liable to be deceived—for his was not a suspicious nature—he was not apt to be. These and other kindred qualities contributed largely to his success, not only in the management of civil affairs, but in the conduct of the war. He was not fretful at just criticisms upon his official conduct, and when convinced of error—which, in his position, was unavoidable —he did not hesitate to correct it. To sum it all up in a few words, he was "the right man in the right place," if there ever was one such.

Some considered Lincoln to have been a wit, but I do not think so, but rather that he was a humorist. They base their opinion upon the fact that he frequently illustrated his meaning by anecdotes, which were almost always appropriate. Many of these have been given to the public, and if I deemed it necessary to the object I have now in view I could easily swell their number. They were the result of memory. He had stored them away in his mind, in which repository they were kept until some suitable occasion called them forth, as if by sudden and unpremeditated impulse, when, without

27

any apparent effort, he made them happily illustrative of some pertinent fact or idea. In this respect he had few if any rivals, and while there was much about this habit both to amuse and instruct, I have preferred to keep fresh in my remembrance his high qualities of statesmanship and his admirable adaptation for the great office he filled under what seemed to me to be providential guidance. There might have been others whose talents and virtues would have adorned that station and who would have clung to the Union with the utmost fidelity, but, in my opinion, there was then no other man in the United States who combined, in so great a degree, the eminent qualities necessary for the crisis. Among these qualities was a sincere, ardent and unfaltering devotion to what he believed to be the best interests and the permanent welfare of all the sections. He never for an instant suffered himself to be influenced by hatred of the South, even during the saddest and darkest hours of the conflict. He indulged only in language of remonstrance, not reproach, but kept constantly before the public mind the great benefits of an undivided Union and the national security and prosperity it alone could secure. His tender sensibilities —childlike in their simplicity—were aroused at the reflection that the necessities of war rendered it necessary that the homes and fields of the South should be desolated, and there was no time between his inauguration and his death when, as I verily believe, he would not have offered his own life to turn away the scourge. If he erred at all, it was the error of the head, not the heart, for in that receptacle of the tender emotions of our nature he allowed no passion or animosity to disturb the dominion of those emotions. He yielded to them in everything he did, and if, as was sometimes the case, the enthusiasts of the North complained of the absence of severity in his treatment of the South, he warded off their censure by solemnly declaring, under a full sense of his responsibility, "whatever shall appear to be God's will I will do;" thus making his own conscience, as enlightened by Divine wisdom, the dictator and guide of his official conduct.

While just men, everywhere, now look upon the administration of Lincoln as having been conducted upon just, conservative and patriotic principles, and cherish a sentiment bordering upon veneration for his memory,—may not the hope be indulged that the prejudice towards him in the South is rapidly disappearing? When this shall be accomplished—if it has not already been—the old sectional lines will be blotted out as if never existing, and the people of the North, South, East and West, held in union by the spirit of national concord, will plant our institutions so firmly that no power upon earth shall be able to remove a single pillar from its base. Then—to employ Lincoln's own words—there will be no future "appeal from the ballot to the bullet," but the union of the people of all the States will rest upon such foundations that no time shall come, in all the future of the nation, for funereal ceremonies at the grave of constitutional and popular liberty.

INDEX.

(421)

28

180, 181; petitions to abolish, in the House, 181–183; relations of, to annexation of Texas, 226, 229, 252, 261, 262, 288, 290, 294; Taylor's attitude towards, 306–309; Fillmore's attitude toward, 314 *et seq.;* establishment of, in Kansas, sought by Buchanan, 365, 366; Buchanan opposed to principle of, 366; extension of, into the Territories opposed by Lincoln, 395; extension of, into the Territories, discussed by Webster and Calhoun, 397; the territorial controversy about, led to the war, 408.

Slave States demanded *immediate* annexation of Texas, 226, 245, 248, 249, 252.

Slave trade always opposed in Virginia, 149.

Slidell, John, sent as minister to Mexico, 274; rejected by Mexico, 274, 275.

Sloat, Commodore, captured Monterey, 283.

Smith, Robert, resigned as Secretary of State, 75.

Smith, Truman, conversation with, about Tyler's veto of bank bill, 212.

Soule, Pierre, minister to Spain, Marcy's instructions to, about purchase of Cuba, 342.

Southard, Samuel L., Secretary of the Navy, 110.

South Carolina, passed nullification ordinance, 159; nullifiers of, bargained with Polk, 254, 255, 257, 263, 293; passed ordinances of secession, 370, 371, 385, 399.

Southern Confederacy, formed, 385, 399; forts, arsenals and other property of United States seized by, 386, 387; fired upon "Star of the West," 399; leaders of, rejected Lincoln's peaceful overtures, 404; sent commissioners to Washington, 405; Lincoln's communication to commissioners, 405; demanded the surrender of Fort Sumter, 405; boasts of leaders and newspapers of, 406, 407; slave-hold-

ers of, opposed Lincoln's proposition for compensated emancipation, 409; the advance of the troops of, 410, 411.

Spain, difficulties with, in Florida, 92, 96; ceded Florida to United States, 96, 269; relations with, led to "Monroe Doctrine," 104, 105.

"Spoils system" first announced by Marcy, 341, 342.

"Star of the West," fired on by Confederates, 399.

State Rights, inauguration of controversy of, 10; encouraged by Van Buren's administration, 185; party, indorsed platform nominating Polk, 248; during Fillmore's administration, 320; maintained by Pierce, 350 *et seq.;* advocated by Buchanan, 361.

Stephens, Alexander H., Vice-President of Southern Confederacy, 385.

Sterling, Lord, Monroe aid-de-camp to, 89.

Stockton, Commodore, took possession of California and established a civil government, 284–286; explained his agency in California conquest, 287.

Sumter, Fort, surrender of, demanded by Southern Confederacy, 405; fired upon and captured by Confederates, 406.

Taney, Roger B., Attorney-General, 157.

Tariff, provisional act, vetoed by Tyler, 217; general act, vetoed by Tyler, 218; of 1842, passed, and approved by Tyler, 220; same, prepared by Fillmore, 313.

Taylor, John W., member of committee investigating Clay, 113.

Taylor, Zachary, advanced with troops to Texas frontier, 272; took possession of Corpus Christi, 274; advanced to the Rio Grande 275, 277; at Matamoras, 277–279; nominated, 300; his letter to Allison, 298–

www.ingramcontent.com/pod-product-compliance
Lightning Source LLC
Chambersburg PA
CBHW030825270326
41928CB00007B/907